Hemingway's Short Stories

TEACHING HEMINGWAY

Mark P. Ott, Editor
Susan F. Beegel, Founding Editor

Hemingway's Short Stories

Reflections on Teaching, Reading,
and Understanding

Edited by Frederic J. Svoboda

The Kent State University Press   Kent, Ohio

© 2019 by The Kent State University Press, Kent, Ohio 44242
All rights reserved
Library of Congress Catalog Card Number 2019023584
ISBN 978-1-60635-387-5
Manufactured in the United States of America

Library of Congress Cataloging-in-Publication Data
Names: Svoboda, Frederic Joseph, 1949- editor.
Title: Hemingway's short stories : reflections on teaching, reading, and understanding /
    edited by Frederic J. Svoboda.
Description: Kent, Ohio : The Kent State University Press, [2019] | Series: Teaching
    Hemingway | Includes bibliographical references and index. | Summary: "Some-
    times characterized as the most significant author since Shakespeare, Ernest
    Hemingway was an acknowledged master of the short story, with his groundbreak-
    ing style and its apparent simplicity and honesty changing the nature of English
    prose fiction. While in the early 1920s some mainstream editors seemed baffled by
    their subtlety, today his stories are mainstays in the classroom, taught at all levels
    from secondary school through university graduate courses. In this collection, 13
    master teachers from all levels discuss these and other aspects of his work, demon-
    strating how they motivate students to appreciate what Hemingway is doing. In the
    process, the collection argues, one can put to rest the stereotyped view of the author
    as a macho adventurer and, rather, see how Hemingway proves to be uniquely sen-
    sitive to his world. The authors discuss both the most commonly taught and signifi-
    cantly less-taught stories that illustrate Hemingway's concerns. Each has a unique
    point of departure, each a rich and unique background to bring to both students
    and interested readers. For further study or for use specifically by teachers, the vol-
    ume includes classroom exercises and resources, teaching points, and commonly
    encountered issues. Contributors include Peter L. Hays, Marc Dudley, Verna Kale,
    Donald A. Daiker, and Janice F. Byrne, among others"-- Provided by publisher.
Identifiers: LCCN 2019023584 (print) | LCCN 2019023585 (ebook) |
    ISBN 9781606353875 (paperback) | ISBN 9781631013836 (epub) |
    ISBN 9781631013843 (pdf)
Subjects: LCSH: Hemingway, Ernest, 1899-1961--Study and teaching. | Hemingway,
    Ernest, 1899-1961--Criticism and interpretation.
Classification: LCC PS3515.E37 Z6264 2019 (print) | LCC PS3515.E37 (ebook) |
    DDC 813/.52--dc23
LC record available at https://lccn.loc.gov/2019023584
LC ebook record available at https://lccn.loc.gov/2019023585

23 22 21 20 19   5 4 3 2 1

In memory of Paul Smith and Joseph J. Waldmeir,
earlier travelers along this path.

And with thanks to James Plath and Linda Wagner-Martin
for their invaluable advice along the way.

Contents

Foreword

Mark P. Ott

How should the work of Ernest Hemingway be taught in the twenty-first century? Although the "culture wars" of the 1980s and 1990s have faded, Hemingway's place in the curriculum continues to inspire discussion among writers and scholars about the lasting value of his work. To readers of this volume, his life and writing remain vital, meaningful, and still culturally resonant for today's students.

Books in the Teaching Hemingway series build on the excellent work of founding series editor Susan F. Beegel, who guided into publication the first two volumes of this series, *Teaching Hemingway's* A Farewell to Arms, edited by Lisa Tyler (2008), and *Teaching Hemingway's* The Sun Also Rises, edited by Peter L. Hays (2008). In an effort to continue to be useful to instructors and professors—from high schools, community colleges, and universities—the newest volumes in this series are organized thematically, rather than around a single text. This shift attempts to open up Hemingway's work to more interdisciplinary strategies of instruction through divergent theories, fresh juxtapositions, and ethical inquiries, often employing emergent technology to explore media beyond the text.

Frederic Svoboda's *Hemingway's Short Stories: Reflections on Teaching, Reading, and Understanding* speaks to the most important issue of intense interest today: how to introduce Hemingway's short fiction to today's students. These diverse essays exploring Hemingway's short fiction are useful to those new to the classroom as well as seasoned veterans. Written by well-known Hemingway scholars with a broad range of experience from public high schools, community colleges, and large and small universities, the essays refresh our understanding of how to introduce Hemingway's work. Hilary Kovar Justice employs filling in the blanks to teach critical reading and writing, and Patrick Bonds uses reality TV. How to present challenging issues of racial representation in "The Battler" are addressed by John Beall and Mark Dudley; Debra Moddelmog explores the role of sexuality in "A Simple Enquiry." Well-known scholars Don Daiker, Peter

L. Hays, Janice Byrne, Judy Siegel Henn, Fred Svoboda, and Verna Kale provide strategies for teaching the stories of *In Our Time* and *Winner Take Nothing*. In sum, these essays revise our understanding not only of Hemingway but also of how to refresh his work for students and in 2019.

Indeed, this volume demonstrates that not only is Hemingway's work being taught in more thoughtful, creative, and innovative ways in today's classrooms and lecture halls than ever before, but scholars are extending the classroom and taking the Hemingway text into new, exciting places that show us now, more than ever, his enduring relevance.

Introduction

Frederic J. Svoboda

It perhaps goes without saying that most people who are introduced to the works of Ernest Hemingway in a school setting—whether college or secondary—are introduced through the medium of the short story. Short stories represent the author's famous subject matter, style, and method of presentation on a scale that beginners can more easily comprehend than is the case with longer works, whether novels or nonfiction. Hemingway is acknowledged as a master of the short story; few if any courses covering that genre neglect his work.

Usually only one short story by Hemingway is represented in any anthology, and so a clear, cogent, and engaging examination of that story makes a huge difference in whether a student will understand, appreciate, and continue to read Hemingway, whether as an individual author or as a part of the great Modernist movement in literature, the arts, and culture. Short stories are where Hemingway's career first really began to achieve traction—whatever the value of his early journalism and experimental poetry—so a study of the stories tends to bring students into the heart of the author's career and concerns. Most of his important stories appeared from the mid-1920s through the 1930s. The stories encapsulate Hemingway's interests: war; expatriation, and clashes of cultures (European, American, Native American); gender, sexuality, and relationships between men and women; changing aspects of the developing modern, post–World War I world; and nature as seen in stories of hunting, fishing, and contemplation. Sequences of short stories such as *In Our Time* (1925) or *The Nick Adams Stories* (posthumous) allow students further to explore the author's work and perhaps to pick and choose their own interests. The stories often are subtle, but because an individual story may be fairly completely mastered by a student, the stories also allow students to use them as springboards into exploration of their own related interests. Perhaps needless to say, the close reading required fully to navigate a Hemingway story is a good preparation for literary study in general—or even for any college course requiring attention to details and the ability to generalize effectively from these.

This collection attempts to represent Hemingway's short fiction with some emphasis on the earlier stories mentioned above.[1] The contributors in this volume discuss most currently taught short stories, but also lesser-taught works that show us more of Hemingway's range of interests and techniques and that expand what is usually thought of as his subject matter. While most of these essays focus on single stories, others take a wider point of view. Taken together, these show multiple ways of using the fiction in the classroom.

The contributors similarly represent a range, from very senior scholars and master teachers to those nearer the beginnings of their careers (and still full of enthusiasm?). Really that latter comment is inappropriate, for all of these essays show their authors' engagement with the material and with their students. Some of us teach graduate and upper division courses, some lower-level courses; others are well-experienced secondary school teachers. Many of us teach in several of these areas. All of us feel the excitement of Hemingway's world-changing literary style and concerns and work hard to help our students to feel this as well.

Peter Hays opens the collection with a relatively early Hemingway story, "Indian Camp," and discusses how it might be taught at a number of levels up through graduate seminars, but with an emphasis on the careful asking of questions that will help introductory level college students to unpack the meanings—and possible ambiguities—of Hemingway's subtle prose. This is literally a matter of "first things": first things in the life of Hemingway's fictional alter ego Nick Adams, first things in the study of the author, and the attention to detail required to understand what the author is about.

Janice F. Byrne's piece on "The End of Something" allows students to explore this classic story paralleling the end of northern Michigan's lumbering era and the end of the relationship between Hemingway alter ego Nick Adams in late adolescence or early manhood and a young woman who proves to be surprisingly independent and self-reliant, perhaps more so than the male protagonist. Byrne's essay is focused on teaching the story to secondary school students with very considerable guidance, though it also includes many elements appropriate for undergraduate college level study. It does not just invite students to understand the story but also to use it as a tool for exploring their own similar experiences and emotions, something that all students likely do, whether consciously or not.

Judy Siegel Henn's essay on "Soldiers Home" engages the issues of homecoming (also seen in "The End of Something") and the barriers that exist among those with different experiences of war. She teaches the story to mixed college classes of Israeli Arabs and Jews for whom conflict and military experience are most energizing subjects (as they also now are to returning veterans of wars in Afghanistan and Iraq), and her experience suggests not only the *how* of teaching Hemingway but also the *why*: what even her technical course students gain from the confrontation with great literature. In addition, her students' status as outsiders to US culture allows them clearly to see Hemingway's critique of his national home.

Marc Dudley discusses issues of race in his essay on "The Battler"—but also the parallel tendency of many college students to try to find one simple answer to a story, something problematic when a multidimensional, complex story explores issues that they might rather leave unexamined. Examination of the story's rhetorical stances and Hemingway's personal experiences are set against the realities of the early twentieth-century world that he depicts, and Dudley concludes, "Hemingway's strange little piece becomes a striking interrogation of race relations at a time when unabashed racial dogma reigned supreme."

John Beall also addresses "The Battler," here dealing with the story, its place in American literary history, and of course its issues in classes aimed at secondary school students. He also uses technological resources to facilitate discussion—and to take advantage of the expertise of university professor Donald Daiker in a team-teaching format to get students into the meat of the story.

Daiker deals with a lesser-considered story, "Cross-Country Snow," as a means of moving his students toward independent reading and self-motivated writing, using class discussion based on short student writings. In doing so, he suggests a little of why Hemingway's early writings were initially undervalued, and how a careful reading can help to make them less so. Taken together, his and Beall's essays also offer insight into how, examining criticism and practice, university scholars and skilled secondary level teachers can cooperate to offer students richer experiences.

In discussing "Big Two-Hearted River," I try to say something about how different students bring different experiences and perceptions to their reading of this story, and to show some of the attitudes—and instructor approaches—that can help to bring them to an appreciation of what Hemingway is doing both on the surface but also in the deeper meanings of this important statement on war. As do the other authors here, I always assume the intelligence of my students, and help them to apply that intelligence to the work under discussion.

Marc Seals discusses what is currently Hemingway's most anthologized story, "Hills Like White Elephants,"[2] and provides college classroom strategies that also are likely suitable for high school use. He interrogates student responses, leads the students through online research in the story's criticism and related material, and ends by discussing how one gets from an initial topic (What is the story about?) to thesis statements suitable for academic papers. As many of us must, he constructs strategies suitable for a classroom combining both sophisticated and novice students of literature.

Verna Kale examines the use of classroom role-playing involving both "Hills Like White Elephants" and "A Clean, Well-Lighted Place." She sees these as stories that can introduce students to Hemingway not as a mainstream artist producing simple, easy-to-understand stories but as a modernist writer who may be radically experimental in his methods and who may produce works that raise more questions than they answer. She also suggests that making fully aware, sophisticated readers is ultimately what such a method—both Hemingway's method and her own—produces. (Incidentally, if "Hills Like White Elephants" currently is the most-anthologized Hemingway story, "A Clean, Well-Lighted Place" probably held that place at points in the past.)

Debra A. Moddelmog somewhat similarly discusses ambiguity in the lesser-taught story "A Simple Inquiry," suggesting that easy assumptions regarding the sexuality of the story's three characters miss the point of what Hemingway is attempting, and that the story encourages students to question their own assumptions and the ethical implications of any easy, stereotyped approach to others. This essay also demonstrates Hemingway's interest in and sophisticated exploration of gender, placed within the context of the assumptions of his time.

Hilary Kovar Justice bookends her college-level introduction to fiction, the first course for English majors—or other students first exploring literature—with stories from early in and the middle of Hemingway's career, "Paris 1922" (very short and not well known) and "The Snows of Kilimanjaro" (relatively long and a subject of much critical discussion). Thus, this essay is not about a single story or even this pair of stories but about how one produces a unified, coherent experience for learners over the course of a semester. Justice explores these stories with students at length, partly to get beyond the trite, last-minute course papers that instructors too often see, but also to help students reach something closer to the richness of experience that professional scholars and teachers find as they approach literature. As in the two preceding essays, she also explores the stories' ambiguities.

Cam Cobb introduces students to systematic literature review in order to appreciate the full range of responses to a story such as Hemingway's other classic long story of the 1930s, "The Short Happy Life of Francis Macomber." Cobb outlines educational theories that will help students to understand the story and then discusses the use of the systematic literature review in literary study. The systematic approach is particularly suited to this much-discussed story, and a technique that all students should master.

Ending this collection, Patrick Bonds makes creative use of a story from the posthumously expanded Hemingway canon, often a problematic subject for those teaching Hemingway. How should we deal with fiction that does not bear the author's full imprimatur? Answering this question, Bonds addresses the posthumously published and unfinished work, "The Last Good Country," another of the Nick Adams stories, and juxtaposes it with the reality TV that many of his students know well, suggesting another approach to ambiguity—or perhaps it is indeterminacy—that can enrich students' experience and make them more involved, active readers.

In all of these essays, we see the richness and relevance to our contemporary world of works of art that appeared almost a century ago, and we see the continual ingenuity and dedication of teachers who bring to their students these works and the issues that they raise.

Notes

1. The most exhaustive consideration of Hemingway's short stories continues to be Paul Smith's *A Reader's Guide to the Short Stories of Ernest Hemingway* (G. K. Hall, 1989).

2. For a discussion of most anthologized stories, including Hemingway's, see Emily Temple's "The Most Anthologized Short Stories of All Time," Literary Hub, 6 July 2017, https://lithub.com/the-most-anthologized-short-stories-of-all-time/.

First Things

Teaching "Indian Camp"

Peter L. Hays

"Indian Camp" is the first story my students encounter in my Hemingway classes after the interchapters (brief sketches between the longer stories of *In Our Time*). I have taught for over forty years at the University of California, Davis, and have taught Hemingway to students in freshman seminars, upper-division lecture classes of from forty to seventy, and graduate seminars. Obviously the lecture classes involve more of my talking, and the seminars more of my asking questions that students haven't already asked and discussed.

I begin by saying that "Indian Camp" is a classic initiation tale: someone learns things during the course of the story and literally travels through darkness to light. In the seminars, particularly the graduate ones, I mention Joseph Campbell's concept of the night sea journey, a quest for enlightenment; some of the graduate students know Campbell.[1] For the undergraduates, I sketch in what's alluded to but not explicitly stated: Dr. Adams, his brother, and his son are on a fishing vacation, the doctor has no medical equipment with him, and, more obviously, the doctor has been called to assist a woman in labor.[2] "Another rowboat" means the one the Native Americans have come in to fetch the doctor, other than the one Dr. Adams and George have at their fishing camp. Summoned on this medical call, the doctor cannot leave his young son alone in the woods and must take him along. To emphasize Nick's beginning in ignorance, I emphasize the darkness, the cold, and the enshrouding mist, all in the story's first paragraphs. Initially I don't ask questions about George's awarding cigars, saving that for later.

1

My first questions for the students are about the state of the story's Native Americans, their abject poverty, the despoliation of their ancestral lands, and their dependence on the white doctor (colonial theorists can use terms like *abject* and *subaltern* here). To get the students to picture the scene and appreciate the state of the characters' poverty, I ask them, Why is it lighter on the logging road, and Why does the young Native American rower and guide blow out his lantern? If the students have missed the implications of the "timber [being] cut away on both sides" (91) of the road, then I explain that the absence of foliage makes it easier for star- and moonlight (if there is any) to illuminate their path. Their guide blows out his lantern to save a few minutes worth of kerosene; they are that poor. I point out Hemingway's repetition of "bark" (92) with two different meanings in order to prepare them for other repetitions later in the course. I ask if anyone knows anything about Native American customs related to birthing, about the separation of the men from the women.[3] Birthing was the women's domain; the birth mother was attended by other women, and the men separated themselves; it was a taboo that operated in many Native American tribes. That the husband is present on the scene leads to a natural segue to discussing him.

We examine what the husband's foot wound might represent. Some graduate students are still into Freud and talk of the husband's symbolic castration, but the undergraduates can see emasculation and helplessness. That understanding is now underscored by their appreciation that the husband is in the women's domain, while the rest of the men, except for the four holding down the struggling woman (three Indians plus Uncle George), have removed themselves, following tradition, and not just because of the women's screaming, as the story states.

Nick's ignorance is emphasized by his father correcting his "I know" with "You don't know" (92). We then discuss Dr. Adams's treatment of the woman in labor: is it clinically professional of him to say that he ignores her screams, suppressing emotion in order to operate as he should (and here I refer back to the absence of emotion in interchapter 3), or is he a racist with little sympathy for an Indian woman? I prepare for this discussion by giving the students a study question in advance, asking if the doctor is a racist. After much student discussion, I point out (if it hasn't been done already), that the doctor refers to the woman as a "lady" twice (92, 93), in contrast to George's "Damn squaw bitch" (93). With this and all subsequent questions, I do not impose any interpretation of mine, but let each student decide his or her own opinion. Student opinion is often mixed and sometimes dependent on the experiences of the student.

But the woman's screams in labor provoke Nick to plead with his father as "Daddy," which prompts us to discuss how old Nick is. Nick's repetition of "Daddy" (92, 95) and his father's use of "Nickie" (94) suggests that Nick is pre-adolescent. A commentator at the 2018 International Hemingway Conference in Paris offered confirmation to such an estimate, noting Nick's willingness to have his father embrace him on the ride across the lake, contact that teenagers are more likely to eschew. Yet Dr. Adams brings Nick to what will be at least a childbirth, possibly an operation—a traumatic event in either case—and asks him to assist. Dr. Adams may be wanting to show off his competence for his son, but is unlikely to bring a very young child to such a scene; hence the boy must be somewhat older. Consensus at the conference was that Nick was ten years old; I might say eleven.

Having already discussed Hemingway's tendency to omit, and thus to compel the reader to supply what was omitted, I ask what preceded the narrator's comment that Nick's "curiosity had been gone for a long time" (93). Most students speak about the trauma of the operation, the bloodletting, about Nick's shock. After this has proceeded for several minutes, I ask what must Nick's reaction be to seeing his father plunge a knife into a screaming woman held down by four men. Is it akin to rape? The impact on Nick must be enormous, affecting his view not just of childbirth (which we see in other stories, especially interchapter 2 and *FTA)*, but of his father. I really want them to appreciate the scene and its effect on a young boy's psyche (and only in the graduate seminar do I include the idea of the castrating father here literally wielding a knife). Nick's "looking away so as not to see what his father was doing" (93) indicates his attempt to shut his eyes to what he has already witnessed, as do the repeated "Nick did not look" at the delivery of the afterbirth and "Nick did not watch" as his father sewed up the cesarean's incision (93). By exposing Nick, even before discovery of the husband's suicide, to a much too traumatic event, the doctor, in the students' opinion, whatever their feelings about his racial biases, is an obtuse and insensitive parent. Lacking a babysitter back at their fishing camp, Dr. Adams could have sent Nick to the Native American men, away from the scene of the operation, but he wanted to impress his son with his medical prowess, to seem large in his son's eyes, as the narrator's description of his "feeling exalted" (94) indicates. He may also have wanted to teach Nick about childbirth, about the facts of life (other than those he announces in the 1933 story "Fathers and Sons"), but he completely underestimates the situation. He should have known that a cesarean performed without anesthetic would be difficult for anyone to watch, let alone a child.

We then move to the husband's suicide and the doctor's humbling. The doctor may have been able to disregard the wife's scream, but her husband was not. Unmanned by his wound, shamed by not being able to help, already abject in wealth, possessions, and social status, the Native American husband is further demeaned by having to summon a white doctor to help his wife. His wife's screams are unbearable, and so he ends his life. The doctor, having neglected to examine the man and his wound on entry to the shanty, now discovers him dead, a suicide, in full view of Nick, providing another shock to the boy, and adding to the quick birth-to-death cycle in Hemingway's fiction (think of interchapter 2, "On the Quai at Smyrna," *A Farewell to Arms*). Thereafter, Dr. Adams's "post-game" exhilaration is gone, as are his certain answers. Where before he could tell Nick decisively that the boy did not know what was going to happen—implying that he did—now he has to confess "I don't know" (95) when asked about the husband's suicide. His subsequent answers lack the certainty of his previous "You don't know"; he now answers with the vague "Not very many," "Hardly ever," "sometimes," and "It all depends" (95). His attempt to show off to Nick has come to grief, and Nick has learned the important life lesson that fathers are fallible human beings, along with the more traumatic lessons he has witnessed that night. Rather than leave Nick alone to face the terrors of the night (as Nick suffered in "Three Shots," the deleted opening to "Indian Camp"), Dr. Adams brings his son with him as an "interne" (SS 93) so that the boy can witness and be proud of his father's life-saving medical skills. Instead, the boy is traumatized by a screaming woman held down by four men, while his father cuts her open. And then, to Nick, Dr. Adams has to confess that there are limits to his omniscience, to his ignorance as to why the Indian husband committed suicide, ambivalence as to whether dying's hard, and even to not knowing where Uncle George is. No longer is Dr. Adams in his son's eyes an all-competent healer, or hero; a process of lessening respect has begun that continues through the short stories to "Fathers and Sons."

So far in my class discussions, and in this article, I have referred to the suicide as the Native American woman's husband; I scrupulously avoid using the term "father" of the infant. In class I now go back to the cigars that George distributed, reminding the class of tobacco's sacred status in Native American culture, its ritual use in ceremonies. Since the doctor and his brother have been summoned to perform a needed service, George has no need to tip the Native American rowers; they are in his debt, not he in theirs. Why I ask, do men pass out cigars? The answer comes quickly: to celebrate a childbirth, usually the child of the man distributing phallic-shaped cigars.[4] The question then becomes, is George the father of the child, and is that usurping of the husband's role another instance of unmanning, leading to the husband's suicide?

Besides the cigars, we have the woman biting George on the arm as he holds her down, and as he looks at his arm, "the young Indian smiled reminiscently" (94). Why "reminiscently"? Is the young Indian rower remembering a passionate partner of his own, or is he remembering a previous encounter of George with the woman. Then we have George's bitter response to his brother's boastfulness, exclaiming, while still looking at his arm, "Oh, you're a great man, all right" (94). Is he bitter for the way the doctor brusquely treated his lover? In the next paragraph, the doctor mentions "these little affairs" (94), then turns his attention to the woman's husband, now dead. When Nick and the doctor leave, George is nowhere present, perhaps vomiting in the woods over the assault on the woman he impregnated and the death of the man he cuckolded, or perhaps staying behind to care for his lover, whom he's already called "a damn squaw bitch." If he is the father of the child, it's another encroachment of whites, another subjugation, beyond the economic, for the Native Americans. I let the students decide for themselves whether George is the father.

We move then to the conclusion. The sun is rising, light is present, and the mists have dissipated. Nick has learned much—and perhaps his father has as well. The bass's jumping, making a circle in the water, refers back to the cycle of birth and death—the fish as a symbol of Christ as well as fertility in the Bible and the Fisher King myth, rising from the dark, cold depths of the lake. Life and death are also suggested by the warmth of the water in contrast to the cold morning air. Unlike the opening, where Nick was in his father's arms, they are now separated, with his father rowing and Nick, a little distant from him, sitting in the stern of the rowboat—a reification of the distance that has opened psychically between Nick and his father. Nick, with all the assurance of a ten- or eleven-year-old, "felt quite sure that he would never die" (95). His sense of immortality has been shaken, but not destroyed. Or he may simply be proclaiming, to reassure himself despite his knowledge, that he's okay, that *he* will not die. And in the next full story of *In Our Time*, despite Dr. Adams's discomfiting before Nick's eyes, Nick still prefers his father to his mother. In "Indian Camp," three whites entered Native American ground to assist the Native Americans; in "The Doctor and the Doctor's Wife," three Native Americans enter the terrain of whites to assist them (the terrain of the whites underscored by the name of the logging company, White and McNally, and by the gate enclosure, initially respected, subsequently ignored). And once again, Dr. Adams is humbled, but that's another day's lesson.

Appendix

Discussion Questions for "Indian Camp"
What is the occupation of the Native Americans in the story?
Is the doctor's coldness toward his patient prompted by racism?
How old is Nick?

Syllabus for Freshman Seminar on Hemingway's Short Stories
Text: Ernest Hemingway, *The Short Stories*, Scribner, 1955.
Additional reading material for Oct. 22: http://en.wikipedia.org/wiki/Fisher_King.
10/1: Intro to class, biographical film, assignment for following class
10/8: Discussion of interchapters, "Indian Camp," assignments for next class
10/15: "Doctor and the Doctor's Wife," "The Battler," assignments for next class
10/22: "Soldier's Home," "Big Two-Hearted River," assignments for next class (optional attendance at bullfight in Thornton, California)
10/29: "The Killers," "The Undefeated," assignments for next class
11/5: "In Another Country," "Hills Like White Elephants," assignments for next class
11/19: "A Clean, Well-Lighted Place," "Now I Lay Me," assignments for next class
11/26: "The Short Happy Life of Francis Macomber," "A Day's Wait," assignments for next class
12/3: "A Pursuit Race," "Snows of Kilimanjaro"
12/5: Conclusion

Notes

1. Campbell, owing much to Carl Jung and the Cambridge anthropologists and their work in comparative religions (e.g., Sir James George Frazer's *The Golden Bough*), describes a "monomyth," the essentially similar elements in traditional hero tales, including a journey beyond common boundaries, often "a night sea journey" (77–95, esp. p. 95, fig. 5).

2. The Indian camp in the story is clearly based on the Indians' bark-peeling camp close to the Hemingway's summer home on Walloon Lake, Michigan. Scholars have tramped the grounds and seen the clearing where the Indians' shanty stood. John, Jim, and Marian Stanford at the 2012 International Hemingway Conference laid out the evidence for both the Indian camp near Walloon Lake and for the Adams campsite at nearby Murphy's Point. That's the factual basis. Whether Hemingway kept the incident there in his fiction or moved it to the Upper Peninsula to separate it from his summer

home and place it closer to the nurse from St. Ignace is still a matter for discussion, although Paul Smith places the story's action in the Upper Peninsula (37).

3. "Tobacco offerings and smoking were featured in all ceremonies" (Kurath et al. 401); "The two most usual sacrifices the Indians offer to Divinity, or the Great Spirits, are a dog and tobacco. Tobacco they sacrifice and strew everywhere" (Kohl 60). "During menstruation and following childbirth, women were a threat to the power of a male. . . . A woman was isolated during these periods" (*Handbook* 715); "The prospective mother was assisted by a group of experienced, elder woman; young girls and males were excluded" (*Encyclopedia* 72); cf. Meyers, 305–6.

4. Tanselle first published on the possibility that George was the child's father.

Works Cited

Campbell, Joseph. *The Hero with a Thousand Faces.* Princeton UP, 1968.

Encyclopedia of North American Indians, edited by Frederick E. Hoxie, Houghton Mifflin, 1996.

Handbook of North American Indians, edited by William C. Sturtevant, Vol. 15, Smithsonian Institution, 1978.

Hemingway, Ernest. *The Complete Short Stories: The Finca Vigía Edition.* Scribner, 1995.
———. *A Farewell to Arms.* Scribner, 1969.

Kohl, Johann Georg. *Kitchi-Gami: Life among the Lake Superior Ojibway.* Minnesota Historical Society Press, 1860, 1985.

Kurath, Gertrude, et al. *The Art of Tradition: Sacred Music, Dance, & Myth of Michigan's Anishinaabe 1946–1955.* Michigan State UP, 2009.

Meyers, Jeffrey. "Hemingway's Primitivism and 'Indian Camp.'" *New Critical Approaches to the Short Stories of Ernest Hemingway,* edited by Jackson J. Benson, Duke UP, 1990.

Smith, Paul. *A Reader's Guide to the Short Stories of Ernest Hemingway.* G. K. Hall, 1989.

Tanselle, G. Thomas. "Hemingway's Indian Camp." *Explicator,* vol. 20, Feb. 1962, item 53.

Hemingway's "The End of Something" for High School Sophomores

Janice F. Byrne

Rationale

Of all of Hemingway's short stories, "The End of Something" is perhaps the most accessible for high school students. First, it is frequently anthologized so that it is already a part of the standard English curriculum in many American high schools. When it is not in the American literature textbook, the teacher or student can readily find it in the school library because it appears in numerous Hemingway short story collections, including *The Nick Adams Stories, The Fifth Column and the First Forty-nine,* and *The Complete Short Stories of Ernest Hemingway: The Finca Vigía Edition.* Second, it is easy to read—at least on a literal level—thanks to Hemingway's short sentences and familiar diction. Third, teenagers easily relate to the situation in which Nick and Marjorie find themselves as their dating relationship deteriorates. Many students in the central United States (where I live and have taught for many years) are familiar with the north woods setting and fishing rituals in the story. Thus they can relate easily to Hemingway's work.

The story serves as a superb example of Hemingway's minimalist style, something students should understand before reading a Hemingway novel. Even more importantly, it addresses the psychological damage to participants in war, what we have come to know today as post-traumatic stress disorder. For those students with friends, brothers, sisters, or parents serving in military conflicts today, the topic takes on deeply personal meanings.

Pre-reading Activities

In my sophomore American Literature classes a dab of Hemingway biography usually suffices to catch the student's attention. With a particularly reticent group, I tend to use the Socratic method rather than straight lecture to deliver the pertinent facts. The conversation usually begins something like this:

> Do you know that Ernest Hemingway was born and raised right here in Illinois? [Oak Park, to be precise.] The house where he was born is now fully restored. Every summer the Hemingway family traveled to northern Michigan to their second home near Petoskey. Some of your families have summer houses in Wisconsin and Michigan, haven't you? How do you spend your time while you are there? Does anybody fish? What kind of fishing do you do? Do you have any particular fishing partners? So did Ernest—and so does Nick Adams, the main character in the Ernest Hemingway's story "The End of Something."

If students are already familiar with the biography, I like to begin by turning their attention to the vignette, or interchapter, that precedes "The End of Something" in most Hemingway short story collections (but not *The Nick Adams Stories*). The vignette begins, "We were in the garden at Mons." I ask the class what is happening in this short passage. What does the word *potted* mean is this context? And why does the speaker seem detached from the killing? I ask them to keep the passage in mind while reading "The End of Something" for class the next day.

Class Discussion Activities

If teachers use the vignette for a pre-reading exercise, it is important that the next class session begins with a reference to that passage. For example, I might write this question on the whiteboard as students enter the room: "From the evidence in the passage beginning with "In the garden at Mons" and in "The End of Something," what conclusions can we draw about Nick Adams?" Once the class has come to order, I give students two minutes to respond to the question in writing. At the end of two minutes, volunteers read their responses aloud. Typically students recognize that Nick has been to war and his experiences have changed him. He tells it like he sees it both about shooting enemy soldiers in the garden and about his relationship with Marjorie. Next I ask the class to write for one or two minutes about what we as readers knows about Marjorie. Again, volunteers read responses aloud. Usually students recognize that she romanticizes the old mill when she describes it as a castle. By this point someone usually comments about the incongruity between Nick and Marjorie's experiences. As teacher, I ask, "What is the essence of their conflict?" Or, "Why does Nick break up with Marjorie?" In the past, this discussion has usually brought students to comment on post-traumatic stress disorder in other works read for class and in individuals they know personally. On two other occasions, however, it prompted students to ask if Nick is gay. He has, after all, rejected his girlfriend in favor of another male. In response, I suggested reading "The Three-Day Blow" as a follow-up activity to further explore Nick and Bill's characterizations.

Here is another way of starting class that has worked for me with this story. The class discussion begins by identifying the basic surface story elements of characters, plot and setting, then moves on to thematic concerns. I divide the class into small groups—although paired partners would work as well—then ask students to list thematic images and phrases in the story. For example, group 1 lists images and phrases suggesting violence; group 2 lists phrases suggesting romantic love; group 3 lists images of the past, and group 4 lists images of food or eating. The listing requires about three or four minutes. Each group then reports back to the class, noting where the images or phrases overlap. Cutting live bait, for instance, is violent, as is the trout's taking the bait. The fish are feeding, or eating, but they will not take the bait. Students may observe that Marjorie likewise does not take Nick's bait as he tries to pick a quarrel; nor do she and Nick eat from the picnic basket she has brought on their date. Their moments of sharing are over. Only the interloper Bill takes a sandwich. As the discussion progresses, members of the class begin to recognize that Hemingway's overlapping images imply the theme of the story—alienation.

Focusing on the setting provides a third approach to the discussion. Because the opening paragraphs provide such a clear picture of the demolition of the sawmill and logging camp, the paragraphs anchor the story in a much changed time and place. From an ecological standpoint, the paragraphs underscore the destruction of the old-growth forest, a sort of land rape that many students explicitly understand. They also depict the annihilation of a culture, albeit temporary, of the logging camp. It was no Paul Bunyan and Babe the Blue Ox kind of place. It was a masculine and often brutal encampment. To Marjorie, the ruins of the old sawmill are like a castle in a Disney production—fantasy. Although the author does not tell us what Nick thinks of it, an argument by analogy will lead students to recognize the metaphor of warfare. Some sample questions for this line of discussion include: How is a logging camp like an army in the field? What kinds of tools or weapons do loggers use that are like the tools and weapons soldiers use? What is the purpose of a castle? Has Nick ever seen a real castle? Has Marjorie? How does a battle destroy the landscape? How does a logging operation do the same? (Students who have watched the television reality show *Swamp Loggers* may speak on this issue as might students enrolled in the school's ecology course.) The story takes place ten years after the schooner hauled away the milling machinery. How long does it take for the land to recover from logging operations? From war? If Nick is like the landscape, how long might it take him to recover?

To end the "setting as metaphor" discussion, sometimes I allow students to sketch one scene in the story. They enjoy drawing with colored markers on sheets of newsprint, with four or five classmates in a group. Usually one will do the actual drawing, a second and third will color, the remaining serve as task masters or commentators. The completed artwork goes up on the wall, just as if it were kindergarten, not high school. The students enjoy these activities and the drawings become useful aids for visual learners, particularly when students with special needs are mainstreamed into the regular classroom

Post-discussion Activities

Numerous student-centered post-reading or discussion activities present themselves for "The End of Something." Here are few from which I allow my students to choose.

1. Read "The Three-Day Blow." Then write an essay of comparison and contrast in which you analyze the characters of Nick and Bill as they appear in the two short stories.
2. Read "Soldier's Home." Then in a short essay discuss whether Krebs and Nick are both guilty of hurting people who love them.
3. Read "Big Two Hearted River." Then in a two- to three-page essay compare the fishing techniques in the two short stories. As an alternative to the essay, you may present a five-minute talk to the class.
4. With two friends produce a ten-minute film version of "The End of Something" to be shown in class.
5. Read Tim O'Brien's short story "The Things They Carried." Either discuss in a short essay or present a speech to the class about how Norman Bowker's post-Vietnam experience was like Nick Adams's post–World War I experience.
6. Interview a soldier who has returned from Iraq or Afghanistan. What

were his or her primary duties? Did he or she see combat? What steps are now being taking to help returning troops deal with PTSD? Write your report as a newspaper feature article.

7. Research the logging industry in northern Michigan in the early twentieth century and the early twenty-first century. Summarize your findings in a two- to three-page report.

8. Visit www.MichiganHemingwaySociety.org to learn more about the Horton Bay area during the early twentieth century. Design a travel brochure advertising some of the spots the young Ernest Hemingway probably visited.

9. Visit a Hemingway site near where you live or vacation. Write a news article about the place and illustrate it with your own photographs. (For my students, Oak Park, Illinois, and Key West, Florida, are favorites. Others may visit European sites.)

10. In a three-page essay, define Hemingway's iceberg theory and evaluate how well "The End of Something" illustrates the theory.

Conclusion

My experience in teaching "The End of Something" has been positive no matter which approach I elect for a given class. I hope that the teaching techniques discussed here help other educators and their students to enjoy Hemingway's short fiction as my students and I have.

The Education of Harold Krebs, or Approaching Ernest Hemingway's "Soldier's Home" with Engineering Students in Israel

Judy Siegel Henn

What is the use of a university without literature? Why teach literature to men and women who are majoring in engineering, and how can it be made relevant to chemistry students? When the consumers of culture are young—in their late teens, as are students of higher education in the United States—educators may say that they are instructing them in the ways of the world, preparing them for "life," and exposing them to the dominant culture of the Western world. However, undergraduates at the Technion-Israel Institute of Technology in Haifa, Israel, where I have been lecturing since 2004, are older and have more life experience: most are in their mid- to late twenties. Fully 90 percent of them (men and women) have completed active military service, and some have fought in wars. There are those who would say that just living in Israel is like experiencing a combat situation. What rationale and argument for the teaching of literature can I bring as an educator to a group of scientists in the making?

Actually, the Technion (considered to be the MIT of Israel) solved that problem, by making it mandatory for all undergraduates to earn 7 percent of their credits outside of their major department, thus bringing many students to the Division of Humanities and Arts, where they can choose from a dazzling variety of courses, including ten foreign languages, and approximately one hundred elective courses (offered exclusively in Hebrew), ranging from musical composition, Middle East studies, and cinema and including photography, choreography, and Shakespeare's tragedies (to name a few).

I assumed that students who registered for this elective course, The Short Story in English as the Topic of Conversation, were looking for a framework for speaking in English, which is one of three official languages in Israel—the other two being Hebrew and Arabic—and I was mindful that I was not going to be lecturing, but facilitating. Nevertheless, I secretly yearned for the short stories to "hold out a helping hand . . . [,] guide us toward the other human beings . . . [and] make us better understand the world" (Todorov 25). I hoped to promote meaningful dialogues in the course, largely based on what the students typically bring to their reading: "personality traits, memories of past events, present needs and preoccupations, a particular mood of the moment, and a particular physical condition" (Church 30–31).

I agonized over the choice of a work by Hemingway and rejected stories for being too long, too complicated, or having characters who were too young; thus I rejected "The End of Something," "Three-Day Blow," "Big Two-Hearted River," "Snows of Kilimanjaro," and "Three Shots," all of which I had previously taught in other fiction courses at a variety of institutes of higher education in Israel. I had already taught "Soldier's Home" at least ten times at other Israeli colleges and universities, and the students had always enjoyed studying it, and so I made it the representative Hemingway work in the course syllabus.

When contemplating writing this essay, I wanted to share my personal experiences while teaching students of different ethnic, cultural, and religious backgrounds who study together at the Technion. I had a vague thought that the mandatory military service so many students undergo would make "Soldier's Home" more relevant to them. Many Technion students are officers in the Israel Defense Force and complete reserve duty for up to a month per year (until age forty), sometimes during the course of the academic year. So when I considered the abyss between the Methodist college that Harold Krebs attended in Ernest Hemingway's "Soldier's Home" and Israel's Technion, attended by above-average Israeli students, the gap was significant. Precisely for that reason I felt that Hemingway's narrative of a shell-shocked veteran of World War I would cause a catalytic reaction and might deepen my understanding of the story. I was prepared to experience a new "reality that literature aims to understand [that] is, simply . . . human experience" (Todorov 25).

In Israel, approximately 85 percent of higher-education students begin their studies following two to three years of compulsory military service, making the average age of first-year Jewish students twenty-two or twenty-three. Among the approximately 15 percent of students who are not Jewish, and belong to the Muslim, Christian, and Druze sectors, only a small percentage of the men serve in the Israel Defense Force (and none of the women), making their average

age eighteen or nineteen when they commence their higher education. Many Israeli university students (Jews and non-Jews) work part-time and take out bank loans, and usually complete their BA or BS in three years.

However, at the Technion, the student profile differs: most have obtained the ninetieth percentile or higher in the "Psychometric Exam," which is the standard entrance exam for admittance to higher education in Israel (comparable to the SAT). The course of study at the Technion is generally four years (or even five years for students of architecture). Technion graduates are at the forefront of Israeli industry, high-tech, medicine, and research: over 70 percent of the founders and managers of high-tech industries in Israel are Technion graduates and 80 percent of Israeli NASDAQ companies are led by Technion graduates (Technion site).

Following the first semester of teaching "Soldier's Home" at the Technion, I decided to challenge myself as a teacher by studying the phenomenal student response in class discussions, by using a questionnaire (see appendix at the end of this chapter). I hoped to deepen my understanding of the unique dialogue that had opened between Hemingway's ideas and Israeli students who were in many ways light-years away from him. Additionally, I wanted to upgrade my teaching by examining responses to my pedagogical techniques.

I administered the first part of the questionnaire a week before "Soldier's Home" was assigned for reading, as I wanted to determine if students were familiar with Hemingway. Most had heard of him, though few had read anything by him, although *The Old Man and the Sea* is taught (in Hebrew or Arabic) as a required text in many Israeli high schools. The second part was administered prior to the discussion on "Soldier's Home" in class, exploring students' grasp of the text. The final part, dealing with interpretation, was emailed to students to fill in at home following the group and class discussions of "Soldier's Home."

The initial reactions to the theme of trauma, based on responses to the questionnaires, motivated me to delve deeper, and so the following semester I also assigned students a brief essay (up to six hundred words) on "Soldier's Home." Secretly, I hoped that a majority would choose the "loaded" topic: "Post-Traumatic Stress Disorder in 'Soldier's Home,'" though I felt duty-bound to provide other topics, such as the significance of home, authority, war, and lies. Sure enough, I struck pay dirt with some soul-searching personal accounts from students, though they were not necessarily based on personal combat experiences. Each student was required to attend a private half-hour lesson in my office to assess individual progress and get help with foreign language issues; this provided an additional opportunity to get reactions to "Soldier's Home." One Christian Arab student who had not served in the military related Krebs's behavior to his family's trauma following a tragic accident (Student, Hakim).

The presence of disturbance and dysfunction demonstrated by Harold Krebs and his family were strongly felt by the students, and some even reported negative feelings about the story. One student, who responded that he liked "Soldier's Home," quipped, "It reminded me in a way of Alice in Wonderland when she falls into the rabbit hole" (Student, David). Nevertheless, the most passionate student responses were indeed to forms of trauma. One student related his very personal reaction to the topic of PTSD:

> Usually Koby was a brilliant commander, but this time I don't know what he was thinking. I pleaded to lead the mission against the Hezbollah forces in southern Lebanon, but instead Yan was sent. I cautioned Yan: I am sure the Hezbollah filmed every damn thing I did in the mission, so don't do it exactly the way I did. Remember, they will be ready this time. Stupid Yan. Too much pressure from the officers made him do the same drill. On my way home I was told. . . . In Tel Aviv everything was normal. I couldn't come home and tell my stories, so I took them and shoved them into my stomach. (Student, Friedman 2)

Another student reacted: "As an Israeli I can very much relate to Krebs, since sadly every few years a war is forced on my country, and we are left to deal time and time again with its consequences, especially the loss of our soldiers. Yet even though this is our horrible reality, sometimes you can feel the same indifference" (Student, Gadish 3). Indeed, the places that nurtured Krebs—the small town and the Methodist college—betray him, because they could not prepare him for the experiences he would have in war. "Personal experiences can change a person, and these experiences are more likely to happen when a person is not in his 'safety zone'. One might say that the more a person experiences, the more he changes, making him all the more uncomfortable upon his return" (Student, Tunik 3).

The emphasis in the course is on conversation, so I deliberately do not lecture to the students (though I admit it is difficult to restrain myself). I open the 105-minute lesson on "Soldier's Home" with a ten-minute PowerPoint presentation on Ernest Hemingway's life and career. This is followed by ten to fifteen minutes of general discussion on issues such as American involvement in World War I, early twentieth-century American middle-class family relationships, and small-town life, about which they generally have some knowledge. The students are then divided into groups of five or six (by counting off) and each group receives questions for a fifteen- to twenty-minute discussion, with instructions to appoint a group member who will give a two-minute report to the class.

The groups deal with dilemmas with which I have wrestled regarding "Soldier's Home": the function of the photographs, Krebs's disgust with duplicity, the personalities of his disappearing father and domineering, Bible-thumping mother, his love/hate obsession with women—all receive thorough treatment in the groups, and whatever each student may have missed in his reading, he encounters in discussion. When the class reconvenes, we touch upon Hemingway's use of language: vocabulary, syntax, repetition—and how they enhance the story. These are not English majors; therefore, both in speaking and writing, there is little use of literary "jargon"—a war is a war is a war. I am always sad that I can devote only one session to the story before moving on to J. D. Salinger's "A Perfect Day for Bananafish," but it is heartening that comparisons are immediately made and students are most interested to learn that Salinger almost certainly read "Soldier's Home."

The private conversations, questionnaires, and papers reveal to me that my teaching techniques have led students to read between the lines, to consider the "consequences" of war that Harold Krebs tries so hard to avoid. The word *change* is frequently used by the students. The two photographs at the beginning of "Soldier's Home" elicit comparisons such as: "Before he was complete and after he was broken" (Student, Agam). Another sees Krebs in society: "In examining the first photo, we imagine that before the war Krebs was a social person, whereas after the war not a single friend is mentioned" (Student, Shumovitch 1). Patterns are noted: "The first photo is a reference point for Krebs to force us to think about the 'rigid frame' of rules and religion he came from, and the second forces us to think how this frame is broken in the army during the war (small uniforms, prostitutes, no attention to nature—the Rhine)" (Student, Pinchuk 1). Contemplating the representation of authority in "Soldier's Home," one student wrote: "The idea of authority is shown as uniformity in society [in the first photo]; in the second photo, uniformity has disappeared, and along with it, authority" (Student, Zuri 2).

One student considered the difference between combat readiness for American soldiers in 1917 and Israeli soldiers today: "There is a common saying among Israeli soldiers describing stressful combat situations: 'I just acted like a robot—I did what they taught me to do, and nothing else mattered'; ... [this reaction is due to] a long, harsh training period, designed mainly to achieve that goal." The students assumed that the haste to get American soldiers into the war in Europe meant that Krebs and others "did not have proper training, [causing] Krebs' illness. . . . leading to his decision to run away from his family, his neighborhood and himself" (Student, Kosovicz 1–2).

Students mark Krebs's reluctance to resort to falsity, "Because it tarnishes the clarity of spirit and conscience that were the defining characteristics of his service, rendering it cheap and unimportant" (Student, Khamis). They grasped that Krebs finds maps significant because they "are detailed and clear—you can't get lost because everything is laid out before you"—implying that sign-posts from one phase of life can, and should, carry over to other stages of life (Student, Vainshtein).

It is significant to note that a large majority of the Jewish students, and many of the Christian, Muslim, and Druze students, are not overtly religiously obser-vant. Although religious *identity* is important to them, they do not necessarily observe dietary laws, religious dress codes, religious festivals, and fast days. Nevertheless, a number of students were quite affected by Mrs. Krebs's demands for prayer and obedience from her son. One student astutely observed: "Once he pleases her he knows he has to go away" (Student, Taragin). Mr. and Mrs. Krebs's desire to see their son with a job (as an extension of their Protestant work ethic) is clear: "As Christians they want him to work and not slack off: as his mother says, 'God has some work for everyone to do,' but for Harold the war isn't over yet and he is trapped somehow between the war and reality" (Student, Suzan).

Home, interestingly, is seen in another way: "Hemingway doesn't describe Helen, but has her play baseball, the game whose main goal is to return 'Home'" (Student, Harel 1–2). To remain in his parents' home would be to experience "a second 'war'" (Student, Klempner).

As I read their papers, I began to realize that I had opened Pandora's Box. One student told of her family's method of coping with her father who (at the time of her writing) had been in a coma for three years following brain surgery: "You try to go back to your day to day life but you're in a bubble. You can't touch anyone and no one can touch you. . . . How can you laugh or cry at normal small things when you know what bad really is. . . . To reenter life after a trauma, you have to relearn how to feel. . . . Being engulfed in a loving supporting system can make the difference . . . Krebs was missing that kind of system: who could he lean on when his life crumbled?" (Student, Lee 6).

One student compared his own trauma of telling his father that he was gay to Krebs's retraction following his declaration that he does not love his mother (Student, Roth). My students' trust in me overwhelmed me, and I was stunned by their insight, maturity, and sensitivity. These seemingly callous students, hard-wired to digital media, opened themselves to me, making me wish there was far more time to spend over meaningful discussions of "Soldier's Home."

I have concluded that literature that is relevant to students inspires the strongest reactions and provides the basis for quality discussions. By inspiring trust, students will share their own experiences in writing and in private conferences. This, of course, is far easier said than done, and I have no instant solution, other than to love what you do and to be as honest as you allow yourself to be with your students. Believe that they can teach you something and that they are worthy. Legitimize subjective monologues, even if they are not strictly according to the suggested topics: if I had kept strictly to my rules, I would not have learned how reading "Soldier's Home" prompted a student to relate how her family experienced stages of grief following her father's sudden death (Student, Michalovici 3).

I understand now that the first two parts of the questionnaire (see below) were superfluous, and only the final questions for analysis yielded significant ideas. However, the most important lesson I carried away, from what I have come to see as "The 'Soldier's Home' Project," is that intelligent people look for forums in which they can discuss attitudes, opinions, and hopes. The legitimacy given to the discussion of trauma was a major motivator. It would be better to give less direction to students in the choice of paper topics. Additionally, if possible in the scope of a course, there is great potential in comparing "Soldier's Home" to *A Farewell to Arms, For Whom the Bell Tolls,* the war vignettes from *In Our Time,* and the short stories, "In Another Country," "The Way You'll Never Be," and "Now I Lay Me." The message of "Soldier's Home" is universal, as one student astutely observed: "It isn't really any one war—perhaps just a symbol of all wars, and all soldiers coming home carrying the war in their pockets" (Student, Ofek 1).

Appendix

Below are the three questionnaires administered to students.

Part 1: Pre-reading Questions about Ernest Hemingway
1. I have heard of Ernest Hemingway   YES / NO
2. I have read something by Ernest Hemingway   YES / NO
   If you answered "YES," name what you read: _____
3. I have studied something by Ernest Hemingway   YES / NO

If you answered "YES," name what you studied: _____
4. I would like to read something by Ernest Hemingway   YES / NO
   If you answered "YES," name what you would like to read" _____

Pre-reading Questions about "Soldier's Home"
5. The title means: _____
6. I want to read the story   YES / NO
   If you answered "YES," give one reason why you want to read the story:

   _____

7. I think the story will be about: _____

Part 2: Post-reading Questions after Reading "Soldier's Home" but Prior to Class Discussion
1. The title means:
2. The story was difficult for me to read: Yes / No
   If you answered yes, tell why it was difficult.
3. The story was difficult for me to understand: Yes / No
   If you answered yes, explain what was difficult.
4. I liked the story: Yes / No
   If you answered yes, write one thing that you liked about the story.
5. The main problem in the story is:

Part 3: Questions after Discussing "Soldier's Home"
UNDERSTANDING
1. The meaning of the title is:
2. Harold Krebs is _____ to be home.
3. Krebs likes to _____.
4. Krebs doesn't like to _____.
5. Mrs. Krebs is religious: Yes / No
6. Mr. Krebs accepts his son and his behavior: Yes / No
7. Helen hates her brother: Yes / No
8. Explain why you chose each of your answers for questions 5, 6, and 7.

ANALYSIS
1. Why are there two different photographs of Krebs? What does it force us to think about?
2. Why does lying cause Krebs to feel sick?
3. When does Krebs lie?

4. What is the difference between the girls in Krebs's town and the French and German girls?

5. Why does Krebs want maps of World War I battles?

6. Why do Krebs's parents want him to find a job and get married? What does Krebs think of these ideas?

7. Why does Krebs pray with his mother?

8. Why is Krebs hoping to avoid "complications"?

Works Cited

Agam, Shelly. Questionnaire submitted in *The Short Story in English as the Topic of Conversation.* Technion, Winter 2009–10.

Church, Gladdys Westbrook. "The Significance of Louise Rosenblatt on the Field of Teaching Literature." *Inquiry,* vol. 1, no. 1, Spring 1997, pp. 71–77.

David, Tom. Questionnaire submitted in *The Short Story in English as the Topic of Conversation.* Technion, Spring 2010.

Friedman, Itamar. "Essay on Ernest Hemingway's 'Soldier's Home.'" Paper submitted in *The Short Story in English as the Topic of Conversation.* Technion, Spring 2010, pp. 1–2.

Gadish, Efrat. *"Essay on Ernest Hemingway's 'Soldier's Home.'"* Paper submitted in *The Short Story in English as the Topic of Conversation.* Technion, Spring 2010, pp. 1–3.

Hakim, Samer. Personal conversation. November 2009.

Harel, Tzlil. "The End: An Essay about Ernest Hemingway's 'Soldier's Home.'" Paper submitted in *The Short Story in English as the Topic of Conversation.* Technion, Spring 2010, pp. 1–2.

Hemingway, Ernest. "Soldier's Home." *In Our Time.* Scribner, 1925, 1970.

Khamis, Yazeed. Questionnaire submitted in *The Short Story in English as the Topic of Conversation.* Technion, Winter 2009–10.

Klempner, Anat. Questionnaire submitted in *The Short Story in English as the Topic of Conversation.* Technion, Spring 2010.

Kosovicz, Tomer. "Shell Shock in Ernest Hemingway's 'Soldier's Home.'" Paper submitted in *The Short Story in English as the Topic of Conversation.* Technion, Spring 2010, pp. 1–2.

Lee, Morit. "Ernest Hemingway's 'Soldier's Home.'" Paper submitted in *The Short Story in English as the Topic of Conversation.* Technion, Spring 2010, pp. 1–7.

Michalovici, Maayan. "Before and After in Hemingway's 'Soldier's Home.'" Paper submitted in *The Short Story in English as the Topic of Conversation.* Technion, Winter 2009–10, pp. 1–3.

Ofek, Maya. "The Image of the War in Ernest Hemingway's 'Soldier's Home.'" Paper submitted in *The Short Story in English as the Topic of Conversation.* Technion, Spring 2010, pp. 1–3.

Pinchuk, Daniel. "Krebs' Trauma in Ernest Hemingway's 'Soldier's Home.'" Paper submitted in *The Short Story in English as the Topic of Conversation.* Technion, Winter 2009–10, pp. 1–3.

Roth, Noam. Personal conversation. November 2009.

Shumovitch, Shani. "Analysis of 'Soldier's Home' by Ernest Hemingway." Paper submitted in *The Short Story in English as the Topic of Conversation*. Technion, Spring 2010, pp. 1–2.

Suzan, Ronit. Questionnaire submitted in *The Short Story in English as the Topic of Conversation*. Technion, Spring 2011.

Taragin, Stephen. Questionnaire submitted in *The Short Story in English as the Topic of Conversation*. Technion, Spring 2010.

Technion Student Information Site. 7 May 2010, https://int.technion.ac.il/about/technion -facts/technion-at-a-glance/.

Todorov, Tzvetan, and John Lyons. "What Is Literature For?" *New Literary History*, vol. 38, no. 1, Winter 2007, pp. 13–32.

Tunik, Maria. "Krebs Is Not at Home: PTSD in Hemingway's 'Soldier's Home.'" Paper submitted in *The Short Story in English as the Topic of Conversation*. Technion, Spring 2010, pp. 1–4.

Vainshtein, Lior. Questionnaire submitted in *The Short Story in English as the Topic of Conversation*. Technion, Spring 2010.

Varon, Guy. Questionnaire submitted in *The Short Story in English as the Topic of Conversation*. Technion, Winter 2009–10.

Zuri, Roni. "Authority in 'Soldier's Home." Paper submitted in *The Short Story in English as the Topic of Conversation*. Technion, Winter 2009–10, pp. 1–2.

Reading between the (Color) Lines

Teaching Race in Hemingway's "The Battler"

Marc Dudley

Ernest Hemingway was very much a man of his time; he was also a man of his nation—robust, modern, unapologetically complex. "The Battler" is a wholly American story. Like several of his short works, this tale is unsettling, and therefore wonderful to teach. I must say that I am generally surprised each time I teach it, and the reasons are several: I am surprised by the number of students who have never heard of it, by the number who have never read it, and by the number who read it as everything but a story of race. I teach this story, generally, as a story of exploration, in which Hemingway mines and examines both American history and, necessarily, ideas of otherness.

I enjoy teaching this story for a number of reasons. First and foremost, it is one of his tightest, most mature stories, even as it comes early in his career. "The Battler" is a great example of the oft-noted "Hemingway style" at work—taut narrative, marked attention to physicality, and evocative dialogue. With his iceberg principle on full display, Hemingway is impressionistic and wickedly implicative. It is, I remind my students, often what Hemingway does *not* say that weighs most heavily on the page. However, getting students to see what is *not* there on the page is often the greatest challenge.

All too often, at the sophomore survey level especially, students want desperately to see one answer, one prescriptive, when engaging a particularly troublesome, though seemingly simple text. Students look for the "right" answer in trying to decipher such texts. Or else, they wish to apply a universal reading to a work, often missing altogether the politics of gender, class, and race at work in a text. Surprisingly, many, even those taking a more specialized, upper-level course, like my American Authors course—come to this particular story with very green eyes. Hemingway's texts, often pared down to an impossible gray—and "The Battler" is no exception—make a singular reading nearly impossible. And therein, I remind my students, lies the fun.

Race in particular often proves a difficult lens through which to read a work; and it proves difficult for a couple of salient reasons. First, head-on engagements with race can often be discomforting, sometimes because they are completely foreign entanglements. Second, and because of this first reason in particular, race quickly becomes that taboo subject that sits like an elephant in the middle of the classroom, silently but insistently biding its time while students find their way to it or altogether avoid it. I do not exaggerate when I say I have had many class discussions expressly centered on African American authors—renowned writers like Langston Hughes, Zora Neal Hurston, and Richard Wright—and the race card is never once played by a single student during those first twenty minutes' worth of discussion. What makes this especially frustrating for me, given this broader discussion about teaching race in the classroom, is that these authors in particular made racial negotiation and matters of American social equity a core part of their aesthetics throughout their respective careers; for them, race mattered. This point is often initially lost on many students who either do not see or refuse to see the work as an exercise in racial politics. I think this is often attributable both to ignorance on the one hand, and deliberate, express political correctness on the other. Thus, teaching these stories is a matter of getting students to see the politics invested in the art and of forcing students to recognize the possibility of multiple selves at work in a text. Hemingway works as an impressionist of sorts, painting character and landscape for striking sensory effect; but he also works as a reporter, a historian, and sometimes a political agitator, looking both to document and manipulate truth for optimal psychic effect. Teaching Hemingway often becomes a matter of getting those same students to discuss comfortably what so many are afraid to mention for fear of flaring up latent sensitivities, to articulate what Toni Morrison calls that "unspeakable thing unspoken."

As an easement of sorts, I begin with a general, but germane application of sociological theory to our discussion, segueing from talk of possible themes at work to a more nuanced examination of purpose. Here I introduce sociolinguist Norman Fairclough's assertion that all human interaction is undergirded by personal or communal agendas, that all social engagement is political in nature.[1] The very act of communicating is an act of negotiation; in that act—whether consciously or unconsciously—we convey our wants, needs, and desires. In truth, artists, I argue, are especially often complicit in such social subterfuge. Hemingway's engagement with such subjects as race drives home this point.[2]

However, we get to this promised land of recognition through some subterfuge of my own, as I first engage student comments about the story's "bizarreness." The "bizarre" comments emanate from the scarred, misshapen, or else incongruous bodies we encounter in the text. In likening this story to any number of tales of the Southern Gothic (here, I often point to Flannery O'Connor, a name recognizable to many), I suggest that students read it as a "grotesque" story. Here I pause to define and then discuss the idea of the grotesque and underscore its purpose in literature, in its charge to shock the audience into recognition of special truths. I then ask them to explore with me what this story could be about more generally speaking.

My students often prove themselves to be quite adept at noting and discussing the story's possible general thematics: it is a story about friendship, many quickly remark. Others quickly note the violent temper that marks that friendship. To that end, we discuss it is as a story about such bonds framed within the brutality and violence of the world. The Hemingway universe is often brutal and unkind, I remind them. Others assert that it is about discovery too. A young Nick Adams wanders the countryside by train and by foot and (re)discovers a childhood sports hero. I usually meet this claim with a suggestion about loss. While those losses of the former prizefighter are readily apparent (he is physically damaged), Nick's own losses, I suggest, are never enumerated, but they are also apparent (no family, friends, or personal backstory). Finally, I suggest that "The Battler" is also a story of survival. As the tale begins, the narrator assures us, "Nick stood up. He was all right" (97). In fact, all of the tale's featured primary players are survivors. Nick makes his way through the midwestern landscape—one strewn with jagged edges, ominously dark spaces, and hardboiled realities—to the other side of the darkness so as to live another day.

The story ostensibly has a young Nick playing the part of a vagabond and being discovered as a stowaway by the train's conductor. He is summarily tossed from the train as the story opens. He then makes his way to a makeshift camp inhabited by a wandering duo, former middle-weight boxing champion, Adolph Francis, and his companion/caretaker, Bugs. After openly welcoming Nick into the camp with talk of former glory, Ad rather quickly turns on him in an inexplicable act of violence near the story's end. Ad's companion, Bugs, summarily knocks the man unconscious as he sets upon Nick, allowing Nick to escape unscathed and enlightened. The quieter moments in between are where the story's more salient elements live, and it is here where Nick's real discoveries are made. Here we discover the duo's individual histories and their shared past. Here, too, I tell my students, Hemingway reminds us of our own dark history in the making.

To fully understand it all, I underscore Hemingway's genius in manipulating actual fact in forging his fiction. I draw student attention to the litany of historically informed fictions in the Hemingway canon, beginning with titles at the tips of all their tongues and ending with those perhaps lesser known. *A Farewell to Arms, The Sun Also Rises,* and *For Whom the Bell Tolls* are all narratives steeped in the painful history of war, as are the tales from *In Our Time,* from which this story is taken. *Under Kilimanjaro,* his final fictionalized memoir, has, in limited relief, the Mau Mau uprisings in 1950s East Africa as its backdrop. I then point them to Hemingway's personal experiences as a reporter for the *Kansas City Star* and the *Toronto Star* as further "proof" of his commitment to history in the making. In short, I tell them, Hemingway, like several of his contemporaries, fancied himself to be a realist first. To corroborate my observation, I point them to Stephen Crane and his self-proclaimed "loyalty to the real thing." A few students often chime in at this juncture with observations of their own; and I am often reassured by the number of students who have read his *The Red Badge of Courage.* Where possible, Hemingway, I tell them, felt compelled to see and experience as much of the world as he could before trying to create and translate experience for his readers. And where personal experience did not afford him that sense of intimate and authoritative knowledge, reading would fill that void. Further, Michael Reynolds's *Hemingway's Reading, 1910–1940* demonstrates Hemingway's lifelong investment in things past. A look at Hemingway's collection of war-related histories and memoirs, with subjects ranging from Russian history to the American West's settling, underscores this point and becomes paramount in my slowly mounting a case for this story being one very deliberately about race in early twentieth-century America. In short, Hemingway was hyperaware of America's long and fraught racial history; moreover, some of that history was unfolding all around him in the newspaper headlines of his day.

I bring further evidence to bear as I remind my students that Hemingway was a writer by trade, a craftsman always working to hone his material. Here I show them a copy of a Library Edition of one of Hemingway's most well-known novels (usually *A Farewell to Arms*), with all its attendant revisions included with the "final" version. Physical "proof" of a master artist working through ideas, sometimes searching for just the right words, underscores my point. I further direct them to his many musings on writing in *A Moveable Feast,* his love letter of 1920s Paris years memories. Herein, Hemingway assures us that truth telling for the writer involves one simple prescriptive: "All you have to do is write one true sentence; write the truest sentence that you know" (22). Ironically, I tell them, Hemingway begins writing that one "true sentence" in our featured story by bending the truth to fit his purposes, and here that purpose is a racial examination of his America. The text itself tells us so as Hemingway mines actual news headlines and injects his own fictions to make this a story expressly about race.[3]

I begin this portion of the class discussion by asking a couple of general questions. These questions are meant to acclimate students to the charged environs of a racial topography. I might begin the core portion of our talk by asking, "If we say this is a story about race, how so?" After all, one of the principal characters in "The Battler" is African American and the pernicious N-word litters the story's literary landscape. Ninety percent of the time my questions elicit a trickle response mostly intent on unilaterally branding Hemingway a racist, as students warm up to the idea of broaching the "R-word" (race) portion of our conversation. Yet, even those students intent on making allowances for the racist language will typically "defend" the writer as merely a product of his time. A typical defense might begin with, "I agree that Hemingway's a racist, but. . . ." And the qualified case against a racist author slowly builds momentum.

Taking their lead, I facilitate a dialogue that—at least at its outset—examines the story from this very perspective. Hemingway is, I agree, a man of his time, using the parlance of his day; he is a man of his time, speaking like a man of his time, using the language and epithets of the day that many would have found to be acceptable in his time. But I concede this point only if my students are willing to go one step further and ask themselves one additional question: Why does he resort to racist language, to those epithets so aggressively (why "nigger" and not "negro"?)? Is it just that Hemingway is that racist in his sensibilities? Or is his usage of such language merely strategic? Is it simply for mere shock value? Our initial concession regarding time and place allows us then to examine the author through the bifurcated, racialized lens of early twentieth-century America. This marks a perfect opportunity to engage my students in dialogue about the racial ideas shaping the politics, the economics, the everyday, for many Americans almost a century ago. Indeed, notions of white supremacy were not relegated to the bylaws of terrorist organizations like the Ku Klux Klan; they were ubiquitous on the American cultural scene. I find it striking the number of students, particularly white students, unaware of racism's deep-seated presence in American life, outside of discriminatory laws and Jim Crow. Moreover, while late nineteenth-century Supreme Court rulings legitimized the separation of the races in America, racial attitudes, social mores, and unofficial prescriptives and totemic thinking had roots as deep as this nation's oldest family trees. One need look no further than the writings of Thomas Jefferson for corroboration.[4] Few of my students are cognizant of the many race riots that erupted nationally during the new century's first decades; or the number of racially motivated lynchings committed during those years; or the damaging prevalence of biological determinism and eugenics that shaped popular thought; or the popularity and impact of the minstrel show; or the growing anxieties surrounding boxer Jack Johnson in the world of big-money sports; or the truly galvanizing power and legacy of D. W. Griffith's *The Birth of a Nation,* a film sparking protests and racial violence across the country upon its 1915 release.[5]

Hemingway, I remind my class, lived this history. As an ardent student of history and as a newspaperman whose eyes were constantly peeled for those people, places, and events that make history, he would have noted all the aforementioned happenings, great and small, taking place both down the street and around the nation. As a boy, he would have been aware of the "science" (eugenics and phrenology were wildly popular among "scholars" and laymen alike) of the day.[6] As a teenager, Hemingway would have noted the rise of Jack Johnson, the nation's first African American heavyweight boxing champion. In the years leading up to the 1925 publication of *In Our Time,* Hemingway would have been well aware of the racial strife plaguing the nation. Chicago, I suggest to my students, was the site of one of the nation's worst ever race riots just after Hemingway returned from war; and Chicago, I remind them, was ostensibly Hemingway's backyard, just eight miles from his home town, the suburb of Oak Park. Moreover, young Hemingway lived in a country separated by the color line; *Plessy v. Ferguson* became the law of the land only a few years before his birth. Finally, I concede, yes, Hemingway was, as so many students assert, a man of his times. Those racial epithets would have been acceptable in many circles, including his own. But again, I ask them, what undergirds the aggressiveness of Hemingway's racialized language in this text? In other words, what is Hemingway's principal driver or motivation?

I suggest to them the possibility that Hemingway's aggressive language works as both a false flag and a deliberate directive by the writer; Hemingway has his reader first rely almost entirely upon general expectation, upon personal and cultural biases; and then he subverts those expectations almost entirely. Hemingway wants us first to read the pronounced racial landscape; then, as always, he forces us to read between the topographical lines. In the Hemingway universe, it is often the unsaid that is of greatest import. Here, aptly, a single racial marker does the work of twenty words. I underscore this point to my students as I have them count the number of racial epithets used in the story. Hemingway uses the word "negro" twenty-three times and, more importantly, the word "nigger" four in a story that spans less than ten pages. The two words are used interchangeably throughout the tale and done so with impunity. "Why does he rely so heavily on these two words?" I ask my students. The answer, in a word, is effect. Perhaps no other singular word in the English language assumes such connotative power as that of the N-word. And Hemingway exploits this understanding like no one else, evoking and fashioning images from reader assumption and bias. The word has divided a citizenry, provoked violence and even litigation, and continues to be the source of much discussion. Speaking of language's temporal nature, Supreme Court Justice Oliver Holmes noted almost a century ago that a word is "the skin of a living thought [that] may vary greatly in color and content according to the circumstances and the time in which it is used."[7] This brings us back to our original concession that Hemingway was indeed a man of his times; but I amend this claim in suggesting that Hemingway was a writer very much aware of his times and his countrymen. As Toni Morrison asserts of the N-word's inherent power in *Playing in the Dark: Whiteness and the White Literary Imagination,* "[T]he spatial and conceptual difference is marked by the shortcut that the term 'nigger' allows, with all of its color and caste implications" (71). And Hemingway marshals the associative power of this one word in fashioning the story's primary characters, Bugs, who is black, and even Ad, who is white.

As Hemingway crafts him, each man seems to be an amalgam of stock representative qualities of his respective race. While both men, black and white, are arguably misfits, both societal outliers, there seemingly exists from the beginning a social hierarchy of sorts at work even in their community of two. At the outset, Hemingway constructs each character, both black and white, as type, each seemingly acting within the very tight racial confines of that narrative space demanded of him by contemporary white audience expectation. This is, in action, that narrative false flag of which I spoke. I ask students to tell me about each of the primary players as we meet them, reminding them that first impressions mean much. I ask, "How is Ad characterized when we first meet him?" I follow up with, "How does Hemingway characterize Bugs initially?" I further suggest, as a means of steering the conversation, that our first impressions of each character are markedly different from those we get just pages or even paragraphs into the text. As such, our first impressions of Ad are Nick's own as he, and we, meet his sports hero, still embodying the endurance of Hemingway's "code hero." "Stoic" and "tough" are among the adjectives given by students as we begin this part of the conversation. Following my lead, students quickly note Nick's awestruck reaction to meeting Ad. While weathered, "misshapen," and "mutilated," this former champion, the narrative demonstrates, is a survivor who boasts that while "They all bust their hands on me," opponents through the years "couldn't hurt me" (99). Further, while barely recognizable to Nick, Ad's big reveal ultimately elicits a giddy "Honest to God?" from him. Students then quickly recall how fit the former fighter is, despite his scary, busted form. Registering a heart rate of forty beats per minute, Ad is still seemingly every bit the man he was years ago. Finally, I remind my students to bear in mind, that Ad, the former champion, is white.

Conversely, broken countenance notwithstanding, students are quick to point out that Bugs appears more sinister overall than the misshapen ex-fighter. They point to his express manhandling of Ad when the ex-fighter erupts in anger at Nick as a point of proof. To calm Ad, Bugs slugs him with a whalebone-handled blackjack. Students sense a seemingly latent violence in Bugs, underscoring his having served time for "cutting a man" as further evidence for a case against him. Here I remind them that what we get is a constructed "blackness," and we get this deliberate construction from the outset of the story. We see what Nick sees, ultimately what Hemingway wants us to see. I remind them that very early on, Nick "reads" Bugs from afar, knowing the voice he hears in the darkness as "a negro's voice," and knowing "from the way [Bugs] walked that he was a negro" (100). "What," I ask them, "does 'walk[ing]' like 'a negro' even mean?" This elicits comments about racial coding.

Hemingway shows us for what we are: naturally discriminatory beings, deriving a sense of self by divining and defining what we are not. Americans in particular use race as a principal discriminating (and discriminatory) tool. Pervasive, and often unspoken, understood, ideas of "whiteness" and "blackness" continue to inform American racial politics. It informs so much of our discussions of police brutality in this country. Imagine then, I tell my students, what that racial conversation was like a century ago. Thus, bringing conversation back to Hemingway's story and his portrait of Bug, I suggest that, alternately, running counter to the knife-wielding thug image of our featured black man, is, simultaneously, that of the genial manservant. And, to this point, the textual evidence abounds. Bugs, as we meet him, is all deference and servility, embodied in the "long nigger legs" he crouches upon as he cooks for his two white compatriots. Thus, I demonstrate to students how Bugs quickly comes to counter all that Ad seems to be at story's opening, encompassing two primary racial types haunting the contemporary white imagination: the "savage" brute bent on hyperviolence and the deferential man-child who is simply happy to serve. "Is this a fair and complete representation of Bugs?" I ask. I remind them that this is merely part of the story. How, then, I repeat, is this story a greater statement on race? Or, put differently, what is Hemingway saying about race in America? Hemingway's grotesque tells us much.[8]

Strong pulse or no, Ad Francis is a broken man, and his misshapen face attests to this fact. Further, his broken body acts as a metaphor for a psychic brokenness. He tells Nick that he is "not quite right"; and as my students are quick to point out, he is in fact quite unstable, boastfully calling himself "crazy." When asked to produce further evidence of a man diminished, students begin to see that same pattern reveal itself; they then successfully mine the text for further evidence, pointing out to me Ad's homelessness, his dependency on his sister for money, and his dependency on Bugs in general for his own survival as further proof of his diminished status. I like to wrap up this part of our examination by directing students once more to the text's own literal diminution of this former great, having them note the narrative's repeated reference to Ad as the "little man." In fact, to underscore his diminution, a dozen times this former champion, this former slayer of men, is cast by Hemingway as "the little man."

And if we are to read these characters as part of a larger counter-narrative to the generally accepted American racial chronicle, Bugs, too, becomes something wholly different from the early evocative markers we get as the story opens. My students are quick to point out that he is, in a very general (and literal) sense, the last man standing at story's end, which, they insist, "probably means something." To that end, I add that of the two vagabonds, Bugs is the calm, controlled (and controlling) agent. As opposed to Ad, who was jailed for being a loose cannon of sorts, Bugs is very much in control of himself ("I hear most of what goes on"), of Nick ("If you don't mind I wish you'd sort of pull out") and even of the former fighter ("I have to do it to change him when he gets that way"). Most importantly, I assert, Bugs, not Ad, controls the narrative for both Nick and the reader; after all, Nick learns, and we learn about Ad's inglorious past through Bugs. Moreover, Bugs has the last word, not the formerly great (little) man.

To that end, I ask my students about boxing's import to this story. Why feature a former prizefighter as a principal character? And how could this fact in and of itself lend itself to a reading on race? To the question of the sport, students quickly embark on a discussion of manhood as exemplified in the potentially brutal exercise. Here I suggest to them that boxing, much as was the case with baseball, was very much a sport of national interest at this point in our country's history. And equally important, like baseball, boxing was for some time primarily a white man's domain. Ad's diminution and Bugs's rise then take on special significance, especially when read through the lens of Jack Johnson, black boxer extraordinaire, whose crossing of the color line inside and outside the ring made him a target for white America. While only a phantom here, Johnson's penchant for testing social mores is mirrored by Bugs who admits his affinity for "living like a gentleman."[9] And like Johnson, with veiled blackjack in hand, Bugs quietly threatens to upset the social order. At the very least, with his very deliberate racialization of this short story, I insist to students, Hemingway questions that order.

When read this way, Hemingway's strange little piece becomes a striking interrogation of American race relations at a time when unabashed racial dogma reigned supreme. Students are usually quite surprised when we arrive at this point in the discussion. At this juncture, I have them read, from the backs of their classroom editions of the text, Scribner's own open declaration regarding Hemingway's lasting influence: "Ernest Hemingway did more to change the English language than any other writer of the twentieth century." With "The Battler," I assert to my students, Hemingway cements his stature as modern with a textual exploration that is equally noteworthy for its substance as it is for its form. This, too, is part of Hemingway's enduring legacy.

Notes

1. See Fairclough.

2. I often include Hemingway's *To Have and Have Not* in my Hemingway seminar as an example of Hemingway the "experimenter." That novel demonstrates both Hemingway's interest in hard-boiled fiction and his investment in the sociopolitical (Depression-era economics are in his sights). Some scholars see this novel as an answer to critics who saw him as standing outside the political fray. But "politics," I caution my students, are about more than conservative and liberal leanings; politics are agenda and interest-driven engagements. And in "The Battler," much of Hemingway's politics are racial. Thus, Keneth Kinnamon's observation that "with few exceptions, Hemingway's biographers have discounted his interest in and understanding of politics" could not be any more astute (149). See Kinnamon.

3. Ever the keen observer, Hemingway made note of an actual contemporary news item involving a former lightweight champion fighter, Adolph Wolgast, and his

caretaker in his later years, gym owner Jack Doyle. In actuality, both men were white. Hemingway rather conspicuously makes one of the men in his fictional account a black man. In building my case, I appropriately ask my students this simple rhetorical question: if race were *not* to be a factor for reader consideration, then why would Hemingway deliberately change the facts? The *real* truth of Hemingway's short story then, I admonish my students, quite possibly lies between the scripted lines.

4. See Jefferson, for example. He wrangles with notions of race (complicated by slavery, that most peculiar of institutions) and clearly struggles with how race, very early on, informs the American polity and therefore American opinion. More germane to this examination, in his *Notes,* Jefferson demonstrates himself to be a man whose own perceptions and opinions on race are influenced by those of his historical moment. Enlightenment attitudes already pushed an agenda of white primacy. Doubting black capacity for creativity, Jefferson notes, "never yet could I find that a black had uttered a thought above the level of plain narration" (266).

5. During the first two decades of the twentieth century, America saw racially charged violence in such cities as New York; Charleston, South Carolina; Knoxville, Tennessee; Washington, DC; Norfolk, Virginia; Omaha, Nebraska; Atlanta, Georgia; Saint Louis, Missouri. Some eight miles from Hemingway's hometown of Oak Park, Chicago, a city cited by Carl Sandburg as a model of diversity and progressive thinking as the century began, was no exception. It witnessed some of the worst violence of the so-called "Red Summer" of 1919.

6. Note that eugenics as a science was held in high regard in both Western Europe and right here in the United States, with formal eugenic conferences being held overseas in places like London and, closer to home, Battle Creek, Michigan. Moreover, eugenic ideology would inform discussions of the "Final Solution" in Nazi Germany before the Second World War.

7. See *Towne v. Eisner,* 245 US 425 (1918).

8. Hemingway, I argue, in his "The Battler," writes a grotesque story. Grotesques in literature, traditionally, are meant to shock reader sensibilities, often helping to impart a lesson to readers in the process. If we read Hemingway's tale through this lens, the possibilities are several. And one such lesson, arguably, is racial in nature.

9. Jack Johnson, the nation's first black heavyweight boxing champion, took the championship belt from Tommy Burns in December 1908. He wore a target on his back for the next seven years as America engaged in a search for a so-called "great white hope" to defeat the black champion. Furthermore, death threats would follow Johnson for years, for both "stealing" that championship belt from white America and for brazenly transgressing the color line outside of the boxing ring, traveling internationally and even dating white women. Most important to our examination is Hemingway's personal love for the sport. Hemingway would have known about and followed the Johnson story.

Works Cited

Fairclough, Norman. *Language and Power.* Longman, 1989.

Hemingway, Ernest. "The Battler." *The Complete Short Stories of Ernest Hemingway: The Finca Vigía Edition.* Scribner, 1987.

———. *A Moveable Feast: The Restored Edition.* Scribner, 2010.

Jefferson, Thomas. "Notes on the State of Virginia." *Jefferson: Writings,* edited by Merrill D. Peterson, Library of America, 1984, pp. 123–327.

Kinnamon, Keneth. "Hemingway and Politics." *The Cambridge Companion to Ernest Hemingway,* edited by Scott Donaldson, Cambridge UP, 1996, pp. 149–69.

Morrison, Toni. *Playing in the Dark: Whiteness and the Literary Imagination.* Harvard UP, 1992.

Reynolds, Michael S. *Hemingway's Reading, 1910–1940: An Inventory.* Princeton UP, 1981.

Towne v. Eisner, 245 US 425 (1918).

Hemingway's "The Battler"

Team Teaching and Questions about Race

John Beall

For two of the last several years, I have been part of a team-teaching effort with Don Daiker, professor emeritus of Miami University in Oxford, Ohio. Teaching Hemingway's story in a high school course in American Literature at Collegiate School in New York City, I have benefited from a long-distance partnership with my former teacher at Miami. Together we have taught *In Our Time* and *The Sun Also Rises*. This essay will focus on our experiences teaching Hemingway's "The Battler," in which Nick Adams encounters the disfigured white boxer Ad and the African American Bugs. The central thrust of the essay will be to explore ways that Hemingway's story raises issues of racial identity that are an important facet of the education of Nick Adams. The story led our students to important discussions about portraits of race in American fiction.

My collaboration with Don Daiker began a few years ago when he emailed me offering to team-teach *The Sun Also Rises* in my American Literature class at Collegiate School in New York City. His offer was timely, as administrators at Collegiate had recently asked me who might serve as my outside professional mentor. Immediately, I thought of Don, my favorite professor when I was a college student at Miami University. So we set up a Skype connection, flew Don to New York for two days of face time with my students, and launched our venture. The problem: my classroom that year was quite a distance from the computer lab, so every time there was a glitch, it was a major hassle to call my colleague from IT to resolve the issue. Nonetheless, after the course was over, the students raved in their course evaluations about the opportunity to have two teachers—a university professor and me, their high school teacher—instead of just one.

The following year we got it right. I asked to teach the class in the computer lab, with its fine seminar-style table, and with Jared Eaton, IT majordomo, right next door. We set up a camera, I asked a tech-savvy student to run the camera and record the classes on my iPhone, and we were off and running. Initially, Don asked students to use name cards so he could see who was who, but that didn't work. So I asked the students to stay in the same seat and sent him a seating chart. Again, we flew Don to New York so he could meet the students in person before the long-distance Skyping. That face-to-face contact was extremely helpful, as my students got a sense of Don, whom I nicknamed "Coach Daiker," and he got a sense of them. They also enjoyed meeting my favorite teacher who introduced me to Hemingway, as I was introducing them. With Jared in the wings, and the fine projection screen of the computer lab at our disposal, we were set. The quick lessons I would offer here: (1) in a long-distance, team-teaching arrangement, try to bring the two teachers together face-to-face for at least a couple of days, and (2) have the classroom with its Skype connections as close to IT experts as possible.

By the time Don came to join our class with our study of Hemingway's stories and *The Sun Also Rises,* we had already established that American writers' portrait of racial relations was a central focus of the course. We had discussed Hawthorne's reference in *The Scarlet Letter* to Satan in the forest as "the black man." We had discussed Melville's searing portrait of American innocence on matters of slavery and race in "Benito Cereno." As freshmen, my juniors and seniors in the course had already read and discussed Mark Twain's *Adventures of Huckleberry Finn* and Huck's use of a racial slur. When we came to Hemingway's "The Battler," my students were prepared to discuss the story in those contexts. They were particularly prepared to discuss "The Battler" because Don had led the students' discussion of "The Doctor and the Doctor's Wife" about what the ending of the story suggests about the relationship between Dr. Adams as offering a positive model for his son, Nick.[1]

After Don started the class by continuing the previous day's discussion of "Doctor," I had the students do a "free write," a technique I learned from Don. I asked three different groups of students to write, respectively, about Ad, Bugs, and Nick in the story "The Battler." I allowed students to use their books, and I made it clear that I would not collect their writing. "This is for you," I said, again and again, "so that we can have a really good discussion of this story." My students had difficulty, initially, believing that their writing was "free"—that is, not graded as a reading quiz. One of the lessons I learned from Don is to give students a chance to write in a context free of assessment.

The first student to participate wondered whether Ad Francis had actually married his sister "because the example of Nick and Bill in 'Three-Day Blow' suggested that marriage might get you into trouble." I turned the question over to the class. Another student suggested that they were not married. He quoted Bugs saying that they are no more married to each other than a rabbit. Another student asked about that reference to rabbits when Bugs says: "Of course they wasn't brother and sister no more than a rabbit" (*CSS* 103). I asked whether anyone in the class had anything to add in response to the student's question as to whether Ad and his sister were married. No one did. I responded: "We just don't know; we only know that he was rumored to have incestuous relations with his sister. The story does offer as a reason for Ad's craziness that he might have been in an incestuous marriage. When we get to the Bugs group, let's see if they have anything to add."

Another student asked about the point of the story when Bugs stopped Nick from giving his knife to Ad. He referred to Bugs's intervention when Ad asked Nick for his knife: "Hang onto your knife, Mister Adams" (*CSS* 100). He suggested that at that point Bugs's intervention set Ad off at Nick, instead of going after Bugs. I asked him: "What did you make of that?" He replied: "I thought it was Bugs's way of saying that this man can be somewhat dangerous, and you probably wouldn't want to trust him with a knife." He added: "I think that's what set Ad off." I commented that Ad has apparently displaced the anger he might feel toward Bugs for stopping Nick from giving him a knife and turned his anger toward Nick. Another student wondered whether "Adolf" was Ad's actual name. He also wondered what the significance of the slow-beating heart might have been, as measured by Nick on Ad's wrist, because Ad goes mad quickly against Nick (*CSS* 99–100). The student added, "With a slow-beating heart you'd think he would be slow to anger." He could see how a slow-beating heart would have helped Ad inside the boxing ring, but he pointed out that the opposite occurs outside the ring. He wondered whether the description of Ad's heart relates to his love life. "Great question," I said and asked if anyone in the class had an idea about the Ad's heartbeat. After a long and silent pause, I responded: "Well, let's just leave it at that. Excellent question."

The discussion shifted to the topic of race when the last student in the Ad group asked why Nick revealed his name to Bugs instead of to Ad. He added: "It seems backward, as you would think the white man would be beating the black man." He asked about the repeated references to Ad as "the little man," as opposed to referring to Bugs as "the negro." At that point I turned the students' attention to the first time the narrator refers to Ad by the color of his skin. After Bugs asks Nick if he would like a slice of bread dipped in ham fat and Nick thanks Bugs, the narrator comments: "The little white man looked at Nick" (CSS 101). I commented: "Notice how Nick ascribes color to Ad. He's not just the 'little man,' so race definitely comes into this story." At that point I had a choice: we could delve into the racial issues there or wait until the group focusing on Bugs had its say. I decided to wait, commended the Ad group, and turned next to the Bugs group, asking "What did you make of Bugs? Any observations you can share?"

The first student in the Bugs group saw Hemingway's portrayal of Bugs as "very positive." He saw Bugs as a caretaker who hits Ad because "he has to" in his role as "a peacekeeper." He argued that the portrait of Ad and Bugs suggests "that whites and blacks can live together." I asked this student's classmates: "Anybody want to respond to his observations?" The first response came from a student who was troubled by the shift from the references to Bugs as "the negro" to the "kind of sudden" use of "the N-word on page one hundred one." After a discussion about whether the narrator's use of the word reflected Nick's point of view, a student pointed out that the word recurs "just two lines down" on the same page. He added, "It seemed uncalled for." I asked for his classmates to respond. The first to do so observed that Nick or the narrator uses the slur at moments when the power structure with which he is comfortable is "reversed." He added: "The word is first used on page one hundred when Ad asks Bugs if he heard what was going on." After reading the passage that set the context for the slur, I asked this student to make his point. He did: "I think Nick senses that Bugs is being passive-aggressive . . . using the N-word occurs when there is a disruption of how society usually is. At points where everything seems to be going well, he refers to Bugs as 'negro.'" I thought his insight was so important that I repeated it in my own words: "So your point, if I'm catching you correctly, is that Nick uses the N-word when he senses tension in the room, as a way of consciously or unconsciously restoring white supremacy, if you will."

At that point another student wondered about why Nick would seem to use the phrase "long nigger legs" at a point when Bugs was cooking for Ad and Nick in what appeared to be a subservient role (CSS 100). This student then turned us to the passage after Bugs's long monologue near the end of the story when Nick refers to Bugs's "polite nigger voice" (CSS 103). This student spoke out the word and did not refer to it as the N-word. "Hold that thought," I responded. Then I added in speaking to the entire class, "His point, and I think it's the last use of the N-word, is that it comes after Bugs has a long monologue, and it's a particular kind of monologue. . . . The only thing that I'm going to add to your point, and I so appreciate your bringing it up, is that in the manuscript the N-word occurs about three times as much ("Battler").[2] Hemingway cut most of the slurs—didn't eliminate them—it's a part of the 1920's—it's a part of what a white boy growing up in Michigan who probably never saw a black person in his life would know."

Then came my broken confessional: "The first time I personally ever got to know African-Americans was teaching in high schools. I grew up in suburban Dallas—didn't know a single black person. Moved to suburban Ohio—didn't know a single black person. Went to Miami University of Ohio—didn't know a single black person. It's not that they weren't there, but I didn't know them. And I think what Hemingway is portraying is Nick Adams, having grown up in a suburb of Chicago—he says he's from Chicago—Hemingway grew up in Oak Park, a very white suburb of Chicago. I'll put it this way. Guess what single novel Hemingway described as the greatest American novel." Without a second's passing, a student responded, "*Huck Finn.*"

"That's exactly right," I responded. "And I think he's using the N-word here in a way that Twain used it in *Huck Finn*—as a sign that, when a white person feels threatened, he'll resort to racial slurs." To which a student responded by observing that Bugs seems to be juggling roles in the story in a way that reminded him of Dr. Adams's juggling roles in "Indian Camp" between being a doctor and a father to Nick Adams. Then the student who initially praised Hemingway's portrait of Bugs defended his position: "What struck me is that the positive adjectives 'low, smooth, polite' made it seem like as though he was really getting across to Nick in this monologue." I told him we would come back to that after we heard from "the Nick people."

Then came a student's response, a student silent to that point, whose comments I am quoting at length:

I am going to disagree with almost everyone. I am going to say that his portrayal of Bugs is very negative, and it might be representative of, kind of, racial times in the country because we see that Bugs is first described . . . as someone who is working while Nick and Mr. Ad are sitting down so he's already taken on this role of, kind of, subservience, and as the story goes on, all we seem him doing is catering to the other people's needs. He is there, kind of serving, cooking, and he kind of saves Nick. . . . And at the end of the story he gives Ad a cup of coffee, and it's almost as if he's starting the cycle over again. He knows this is going to happen again, and so it's like Bugs is kind of trapped in this cycle, and he can't really escape it. So that might be representative of what was going on in the country at the time.

My response: "There's just no getting around that." And then I turned to "the Nick people."

The next student's comment was that Nick is armed with a knife, so why can't he be more aggressive. My response was that "One thing Nick learned from his father [in "The Doctor and the Doctor's Wife"] is not to provoke a conflict with someone who's going to beat the crap out of you." Another student reminded us of the passage where Bugs referred to Ad's money and suggested that Bugs is using Ad for his money. My response was that traveling with Ad was the one way Bugs could travel without serving as a Pullman porter, and I referred to "Porter," a poem students would later read by Langston Hughes about that kind of job. At that point I turned the students to Bugs's speech about his companionship with Ad: "He likes to think I'm crazy and I don't mind. I like to be with him and I like seeing the country and I don't have to commit no larceny to do it. I like living like a gentleman" (*CSS* 103). At this point, the student who began the discussion by arguing that Hemingway's portrayal of Bugs is positive now conceded but insisted that "he's just taking care of a lunatic, yet he's living like a gentleman. . . . To me that seems positive." To which I responded: "I think the disagreement between [your classmate] and you is part of the richness of the story."

As we continued with "the Nick people," the next student observed: "I think this is the first time we're seeing Nick on his own in the real world. . . . We're seeing Nick growing up. He doesn't really know what he's doing." At that point I commented about the progression from "The Three-Day Blow," where Nick and Bill are getting drunk, to chapter 6, when Nick is wounded in World War I. After referring briefly to Hemingway's needing to replace "Up in Michigan," with another story, I told my students: "Imagine this collection if you go straight from 'Three Day Blow' to chapter 6. Hemingway wrote 'The Battler,' the last story he put in this collection, as a substitute for 'Up in Michigan.' What the story gives us is the transition from Nick's leaving his childhood home to his being wounded in Italy." After my reference to having mapped out Nick's journey from Chicago to northern Michigan (Mancelona), Don weighed in: "He's heading away from Chicago. He's heading towards the northern Michigan country." I responded with another confessional moment: "I don't think it's an accident that in this story he calls himself 'Nick Adams.' When I was a boy I was 'John.' By the time Professor Daiker taught me, I was 'John Beall.' You get your last name when you become an adult."

The discussion then turned to the ending of the story, particularly Bugs's monologue. As one student observed, "Bugs's monologue almost takes over Nick's voice here." My response: "Which is why I think you get Nick's last use of the N-word as Nick reasserts his white privilege." Then, after explaining how a dramatic monologue is a monologue where the speaker adjusts his speech based on how his auditor is reacting, I read a section of Bugs's speech, ending with "You'll hit a town about two miles up the track. Mancelona they call it. Good bye" (*CSS* 103). In that speech Bugs is directing Nick suavely and clearly to leave the camp. Then I gave my reading of the story: "I think you're right. This portrait of Bugs does reflect the times. But I also think it is a portrait of an African American at the time who's doing everything he can to make the best of a racist situation." To which my student responded: "But, but he's portrayed as more powerful than Ad, but he stays. It's like he has this dependency on Ad. He could leave if he wanted to. He could take the same path Nick is taking and go up north." I replied, "I think that is absolutely a legitimate reading of the story. And no less a writer than Toni Morrison has written to that effect about the story" (Morrison 82–87).[3] Don got the last word, "I thought it was a great discussion. This discussion raised some questions for me, and then helped answer other questions I have about the story as well. Thank you."

As I reflect back upon this class, which took place several years ago, I offer a few observations. First, although I read this story as Hemingway's positive portrayal of Bugs as Nick's first mentor after Dr. Adams, I try to keep that view behind closed doors as I teach the class. I view my role as teacher as opening up discussions and raising questions, not as persuading my students to share my reading of a particular poem, story, novel, or play. As this discussion suggests, part of the power of Hemingway's "The Battler" is its leaving open a multiple range of responses, as occurs when I teach Shakespeare's *Merchant of Venice*. Is the author's portrait of Shylock or Bugs anti-Semitic/racist, or is it a portrait reflecting the anti-Semitism/racism of that place and time? Second, although Don and I were team-teaching the class during the weeks we spent on Hemingway, we were not team-teaching each class as teachers with an equal part in each discussion. Rather, Don took the lead on some stories, like "The Doctor and the Doctor's Wife," and I took the lead on others, like "The Battler." Third, part of the value of my students' discussion of "The Battler" was to open a discussion of race in America that included works by Langston Hughes, James Baldwin, and Octavia Butler. Had the course begun or ended with Hemingway, I do not think it would have been rightly titled "American Literature." Two excerpts from my students' final-exam essays should illustrate this point:

Excerpt 1: In "This Morning, This Evening, So Soon" and in *Kindred,* both James Baldwin and Octavia Butler use an interracial marriage to explore the racial prejudice of America's past, but through very different styles and narrative perspectives. Baldwin uses Paul, the product of the interracial marriage between the narrator and Harriet, to make the narrator reflect on his time in the United States and consider whether Paul will be able to escape the racial prejudice the narrator faced.

Excerpt 2: James Baldwin's short story, "Going to Meet the Man" and Herman Melville's novella, "Benito Cereno," focus on two main themes: the cruel institution of slavery and the racial oppression of freed African Americans. Both stories are told from the limited third-person point of view. Melville's story is narrated from the perspective of the protagonist Amasa Delano, a white sea captain. Baldwin, however, narrates his story from the point of view of the man he would have most despised—a racist, southern deputy sheriff named Jesse.

Hemingway's story "The Battler" opened important questions of racial identity and tension that led to the students' continued consideration of these difficult issues.

In their written, anonymous evaluations at the end of course, every single one of my students singled out the team-teaching aspect of the course as important to retain in future classes. Most of these comments came in response to the final question I posed: "Are there aspects of the course that you recommend your teacher to retain? That your teacher should change?" In response, one student wrote: "I would recommend to return to the joint class discussions with Professor Daiker." Another commented: "The classes with Daiker were great. Definitely keep those." Likewise, a third student wrote: "Keep Skyping with Dr. Daiker." One student commented on the benefit of having two teachers leading discussions on the same works of literature: "The classes with Professor Daiker were very interesting and I enjoyed having the opinions of a second teacher for a good portion of the semester." And so on. This team-teaching arrangement is highly unusual in my school. Thus, one student who answered my final question with a recommendation for change wrote: "More classes with Don Daiker and more Hemingway."

Appendix: Comments from Donald Daiker

Teaching Hemingway with John Beall in person and via Skype has been one of the most rewarding experiences of my academic life. What a pleasure to discuss Hemingway's fiction in detail with a dozen very bright, very committed, and very articulate students in the presence of an instructor who respects his students, encourages their voices, and welcomes questions and intellectual challenges.

The classroom I know best is one where the instructor closes the classroom door—either literally or metaphorically—and where only the instructor speaks with the weight and clout of authority. In my earlier years at Miami University I remember asking the most popular instructor in the English Department if I might be able to visit his classroom to learn how to teach from him, but he declined because he said my presence might disturb the "equilibrium" of his classroom. But when John and I are together in his Collegiate School classroom, we occasionally like to stir things up, sometimes by disagreeing profoundly if cordially. I know that John questions my reading of "Indian Camp" and "The Doctor and the Doctor's Wife" because he thinks I give far too much credit to Dr. Adams as a positive model for his son. By the same token, I question his take on the character Sam in "The Killers." John sees Sam, like Bugs in "The Battler," as an example of good behavior, whereas I see him—along with George and Ole Anderson (and Uncle George in "Indian Camp" and Bill in "The Three-Day Blow")—as offering bad, irresponsible models for the young, impressionable Nick.

For high school juniors and seniors to see two instructors they respect and perhaps even admire disagreeing with each other over fundamental questions of interpretation is a valuable and, in this complex world, necessary lesson.

For me, to sit across the room from John as we each offer contrasting and perhaps even mutually exclusive interpretations of not only a key passage but an entire story—what a humbling but exciting learning experience that is!

Outside of the classroom I continue learning from John—through his presentations in Venice, East Lansing, and Oak Park as well as through the results of his original research at Princeton, the New York Public Library, and the Hemingway Room of the John F. Kennedy Library that appear in journals like *The Hemingway Review,* the *James Joyce Quarterly,* and *MidAmerica.*

Notes

1. One of my students recorded each of the classes I team-taught with Don. I posted those recordings on the website I set up for the course. For Don's recent essay on "The Doctor and the Doctor's Wife," see Daiker, 45–65. For supporting Don's role as my coach, co-teacher, and collaborator, I would like to thank Dr. Lee Levison, headmaster, and Dr. Bill Bullard, former academic dean, at the Collegiate School.

2. In my classes of American literature, my students and I are uncomfortable using the N-word in reading aloud from the texts, whether the author is Twain, Hemingway, Baldwin, or Morrison. Near the end of the course, the students read the racial slur in as gruesome a context as I can imagine in Baldwin's title story in his collection *Going to Meet the Man.* I do not forbid students from reading the word aloud so long as we discuss its implications.

3. See also Dudley, 69–81; Wright-Cleveland in Holcomb and Scruggs, 160–162; and Marshall in Holcomb and Scruggs, 200–204. For a different reading of Hemingway's portrait of Bugs, see Holcomb, "Race and Ethnicity." Holcomb sees Bugs as "a kin of Invisible Man's grandfather, . . . a character who reflects the disobedient New Negro" (311–12). Also see Beall, "Bugs and Sam."

Works Cited

Baldwin, James. *Going to Meet the Man.* Vintage, 1995.

Beall, John. "Bugs and Sam: Nick Adams's Guides in Hemingway's 'The Battler' and 'The Killers.'" *Hemingway Review,* vol. 38, no. 2, Spring 2019, pp. 42–58.

Butler, Octavia E. *Kindred.* Beacon Press, 2003.

Daiker, Donald A. "Defending Hemingway's Doctor Adams: The Doctor, the Critics, and the Doctor's Son." *Middle West Review,* vol. 3, no. 2, Summer 2017, pp. 45–65.

Dudley, Marc K. *Hemingway, Race, and Art: Bloodlines and the Color Line.* Kent State UP, 2011.

Hemingway, Ernest. "The Battler" (typescript titled "The Great Man"), Ernest Hemingway Collection, John F. Kennedy Library, box 27, folder 269.

———. *The Complete Short Stories of Ernest Hemingway.* Scribner, 2003.

Holcomb, Gary Edward. "Race and Ethnicity: African Americans." *Ernest Hemingway in Context,* edited by Debra A. Moddelmog and Suzanne Del Gizzo, Cambridge UP, 2015, pp. 307–14.

Holcomb, Gary Edward, and Charles Scruggs. *Hemingway and the Black Renaissance.* Ohio State UP, 2012.

Hughes, Langston, et al. *The Collected Poems of Langston Hughes.* Vintage, 1995.

Melville, Herman. *Billy Budd and Other Tales.* New American Library, 1979.

Morrison, Toni. *Playing in the Dark: Whiteness and the Literary Imagination.* Vintage, 1993.

Twain, Mark. *Adventures of Huckleberry Finn: Tom Sawyer's Comrade,* edited by Victor Fischer and Lin Salamo, U of California P, 2001.

Wright-Cleveland, Margaret E. "*Cane* and *In Our Time.*" *Hemingway and the Black Renaissance,* edited by Gary Edward Holcomb and Charles Scruggs, Ohio State UP, 2012, pp. 151–76.

Teaching Hemingway's "Cross-Country Snow"

Donald A. Daiker

This story "just infuriated me with its superficiality," a high school junior honors student wrote after reading Ernest Hemingway's "Cross-Country Snow." Even an experienced Hemingway reader like Paul Smith found the story "trivial," more like "an unfinished exercise" than a full-bodied story deserving of serious critical attention (84). These comments suggest that a central challenge in teaching Hemingway's fiction of the mid-1920s—not only short stories like "Cross-Country Snow" and "Big Two-Hearted River" from *In Our Time* (1925) but the novel *The Sun Also Rises* (1926) as well—may be helping students see that these early works are anything but the simple, superficial, and straightforward narratives they may initially seem.

Before Hemingway established his reputation with the publication of *The Sun Also Rises,* his short stories were routinely rejected by journal editors because they seemed to be superficial—to lack weight and substance, to be less than stories. In his memoir *Green Hills of Africa,* Hemingway recalls, from his Paris days of the early to mid-1920s, "all of the stories back in the mail that came in through a slit in the saw-mill door, with notes of rejection that would never call them stories, but always anecdotes, sketches, contes, etc. They did not want them" (*GHOA* 70). The challenge for teachers, then, is to create a classroom environment that encourages students to see beneath the placid surface of a Hemingway story into the depths below.[1]

In my own classes such encouragement begins with an out-of-class writing assignment—like the one below—to be completed and submitted[2] *before* the story is first discussed.

After reading "Cross-Country Snow," write an essay of about 250 words in response to ONE (only one) of the topics below:

1. Some readers think "Cross-Country Snow" is a trivial and superficial story. Other readers think it presents much of Hemingway's philosophy of life. What do you think and why?

2. Are Nick and George good friends or not? Why do you think so? Be very specific.

3. What for you is the TONE of "Cross-Country Snow"? Is it happy? sad? funny? bitter? cheerful? somber? optimistic? pessimistic? what? Be very specific in supporting your position.

The purposes of such a pre-discussion writing assignment are many. The questions themselves are designed to make clear to students that there is no one right way of interpreting the story, that past readers have differed substantially in their responses. The questions are worded—"What do *you* think" and "What for *you*"—so as both to underscore these differences and to valorize the student's unique response. The assignment itself requires students to engage in the vital act of writing and, by addressing a key issue, to become intellectually and perhaps even emotionally engaged with the story, thus enhancing chances for learning as well as for lively class discussion. If collected or checked,[3] the assignment not only encourages students actually to read the assigned story but provides the instructor with evidence of student work and with material for classroom use. Often in my own college courses—Introduction to Literature, American Literature, the Short Story—I ask two or three students, on a rotating or extra-credit basis, to submit their writing before class so that I can duplicate it for their classmates. Here is one such response to question 2 above from Ben Whiteman, a high school junior honors student:

"Cross-Country" Snow Response
The question of whether or not Nick and George are friends is not a difficult one. Hemingway makes the reader work harder than most authors: forcing us to investigate his diction and make inferences based upon minute changes in dialogue in order to discover the true meaning of the piece.

The first thing that jumps out at the reader is the fact that George addresses Nick as "Mike." At first we are perplexed by this mistake, but as we read further we find that Nick calls George by the name of "Gidge," which leads us to realize these must be nicknames. Shortly thereafter, Nick offers that they ski together, however George declines and says, "No, you come on and go first. I like to see you take the khuds" (*CSS* 143). George must have skied with Nick before, and admires his ability to maneuver about the hills.

The next clue we have as to the friendship between these two men appears when they arrive at the inn to warm up. The two sit down at a table, and the barmaid asks what they would like to drink. Nick replies, asking for a bottle of Sion. He verifies that this is fine with George, who confirms the choice and goes on to remark, "You know more about wine than I do. I like any of it" (144). Later on, Hemingway is uncharacteristically straightforward and tells us that they are fond of each other, and that each was content in the company of the other.

Finally, George inquires into the pregnancy of Helen, whom we can only assume is Nick's wife. Such a familiarity with Nick's spouse is very telling of the length of their friendship. The majority of the final page is a conversation that most would amount to small talk, and there is a feeling of awkwardness which might lead some to say the two are uncomfortable around each other. However if we relate the previous events and dialogue to this, we can conclude that these two have been friends for so long that speech is nothing but a ceremonial form of communication. These two know so much about each other that they can express themselves in ways that are not verbal, and yet each knows enough about the other to understand.

Ben Whiteman

It's vitally important, of course, that student writing be shared with classmates. In my college courses I ask students to provide copies. In high school, I do the copying myself. Either way, students follow the written copy before them as it is read aloud by the student writer. This structure thus places the student's voice, both written and oral, at the starting center of discussion, one of several strategies for decentering myself in the classroom and conferring proprietary rights to students, whose experiences in reading and responding to the academic writing of their classmates is usually quite limited, often only to school literary magazines. Once the response is read aloud and the student writer is thanked, the instructor chooses where to go next. If there are hands waving or if body language reveals that students are eager to respond, that's usually where I'll go. If not, following the advice of master teacher Don Murray, I often proceed by asking two key questions about the student essay: (1) What works? and (2) What needs work? The question "What works?" can apply to the writing itself or to the interpretation of "Cross-Country Snow" that it presents. If my day's primary focus is on Hemingway's story rather than writing about fiction, I would ask Ben's classmates if they are convinced by his argument that Nick and George are good friends. I might even call for a show of hands to make sure everyone is participating in some way. I would certainly ask what Ben said that worked, that helped convince them of the friendship.

In response, a student might point to Ben's assertion that the use of nicknames—"Mike" and "Gidge"—suggests close friendship, an assertion made more credible because Ben had considered, before finally rejecting, the notion that George's calling Nick "Mike" is a mistake. In fact, one of Ben's classmates had written that it was indeed a mistake and thus a demonstration that the two skiers are not close friends at all.[4] Following class discussion, I would have to decide whether to call attention to one of George's last statements in the story: "'Maybe we'll never go skiing again, Nick,' George said" (CSS 146). Here, when George becomes nostalgic, philosophical, and serious, he does not make the same "mistake" as earlier: he dispenses with the playful "Mike" and addresses Nick by his given name.

Ben's written response to "Cross-Country Snow" functions not only to generate class discussion about the story's meaning and significance. It also places Ben, albeit temporarily, in the position of class teacher—with classmates reading and listening to his words and learning from them as well. They learn from Ben that "Hemingway makes the reader work harder than most authors" (No, I don't know how Ben got to be so smart!). They learn—or at least get to consider—that the friends' conversation at the inn may be "a ceremonial form of communication." Now Ben may be a more perceptive reader than most, but sharing writing in the classroom allows students to function as the teachers of their fellow students, particularly if the instructor points to especially insightful or provocative passages in the student writing. In *The Sun Also Rises,* the novel Hemingway began the year "Cross-County Snow" was published, Jake Barnes becomes the student—first, of Count Mippipopolous and then, with more enduring consequences, of the bullfighter Pedro Romero—learning his lessons so well that he teaches them to Lady Brett Ashley and, with much greater success, to himself.[5]

I might next ask students if they think the theme of friendship is important to "Cross-Country Snow" and in this way approach the issue of the story's superficiality. Aside from citing Ben's additional examples—familiarity with the other's skiing patterns, George's knowledge of Nick's wife Helen, comfort in each other's company, and Hemingway's direct statement that "They were fond of each other" (CSS 145)—students might point to the noncompetitive nature of the friendship, to the alternating leadership (George on the slopes,

Nick at the inn), and to instances of mutual support: Nick's holding down the top stand of the wire fence so that George can slide over it and their slapping snow off each other's trousers before entering the inn (144).

My students have heard me say, more than once, that the first and last lines—and sometimes the first and last words—of any work are often unusually significant. This is especially true for Hemingway: "In the early morning on the lake sitting in the stern of the boat with his father rowing, he felt quite sure that he would never die" (*CSS* 70); "There were plenty of days coming when he could fish the swamp" (*CSS* 180); and "'Yes.' I said. 'Isn't it pretty to think so?'" (*SAR* 249). So I would hope that a student would cite the story's final line: "Now they would have the run home together" (*CSS* 147). If so, I would be sure to ask, "Well, do you think the story's final word—'together'—is especially important?" I would hope at least one student would assert that "together" nicely reinforces and clinches the theme of friendship—the warmth and value of human companionship—that emerges from the story.

Is the theme of friendship, which appears also with Nick and Bill in "The End of Something" and "The Three-Day Blow," both from *In Our Time,* and with Jake Barnes and Bill Gorton in *The Sun Also Rises,* sufficient to redeem "Cross-County Snow" from charges of triviality and superficiality? Perhaps not. So I might ask my students to turn next to the story's opening sentence and particularly its second word: "The funicular car bucked once more and then stopped" (*CSS* 143).

This might be a good time to do what I frequently do: ask students to write briefly in class about a problematic line or paragraph. "Take about a minute and write down what you think is the importance of this opening line. I will not collect your writing, but after a minute I will ask you to read what you've written to the person sitting next to you." After students have written and shared their writing, after I've asked for volunteers to read their writing aloud, and after we've established that Nick is on a skiing trip in a yet-undefined location, I will want to focus on connections between the opening sentence and the rest of the story.

What the opening sentence makes clear is the presence and power of limitations: the funicular car cannot reach the top of the ski slope because the snow has drifted solidly across its path to the summit. It is but the first of many barriers and obstacles that limit what is possible. There is the unexpected "patch of soft snow" (143) that causes both Nick and George to fall. There is the "fence"—mentioned three times—that forces Nick and George to turn sharply rightward on the second slope. There is the road of "polished ice" (144) that makes the skiers keep to the stretch of roadside snow. But there are barriers and limitations inside the inn as well as on the slopes. Their enjoyment of wine is limited by "specks of cork" (145)—despite Nick's wanting to believe that they "don't matter"—and by George's feeling "funny" after a single bottle of Sion. Most notably, their desire to "just bum together" (145), backpacking and skiing through the Swiss and German countryside, is limited by life's practicalities and responsibilities: George must return to school and Nick must return to the United States with his pregnant wife. Although some readers interpret "Cross-Country Snow" as either the glorification or condemnation of freedom and youthful escape from adult responsibility, the presence throughout of barriers and obstacles make clear that the pleasures of skiing and friendship that Nick and George enjoy are earned in the context of life's inevitable restrictions.

So why does Hemingway begin his story with "The funicular car"? And what is *funicular* anyway? Because there are often skiers in my class, at least one student usually knows, and can tell the rest of us, what a funicular car is and how it differs from an ordinary ski lift.[6] Whereas according to the *American Heritage Dictionary* a ski lift is a "power-driven conveyer, usually with attached towing bars, suspended chairs, or gondolas, used to carry skiers to the top of a trail or slope," a funicular lift—by contrast—is a "cable railway on a steep incline, esp. such a railway with simultaneously ascending and descending cars counterbalancing each other." The question for the class then becomes, Does the funicular car function as a metaphor in the story? Is "Cross-County Snow," like the lift itself, about counterbalancing forces? Perhaps it's enough, at this point, to leave the question unanswered, to suggest to students that counterbalance, or reciprocity, is a promising topic for a longer paper (possibly to be included in the course portfolio, which replaces the traditional final examination in all my classes).

With writers in general and with famous authors like Fitzgerald, Plath, Salinger, and Hemingway in particular, students are often understandably curious about the autobiographical basis of the fiction they read. So at some stage of our discussion, I might quickly convey what I have learned from Hemingway's finest biographers—Carlos Baker and Michael Reynolds. Ernest Hemingway and his wife, Hadley, spent a month during the winters of 1922 and 1923, when he was twenty-two and twenty-three, skiing and bobsledding in Chamby sur Montreux, Switzerland. One of their skiing companions was George O'Neil, nicknamed Gidge, the seventeen-year-old son of a retired American businessman who had come to Europe to write poetry. Although the Hemingways practiced birth control, Hadley became pregnant in January 1923, and soon afterwards she and Ernest decided to return to North America—to Toronto, Canada, rather than "the States" (*CSS* 146)—for the birth of their child.

But what seems far more useful to understanding "Cross-Country Snow" than these biographical facts is Hemingway's long feature story that appeared in the December 22, 1923, issue of the *Toronto Star Weekly*. Titled "Christmas on the Roof of the World," this remarkable dispatch echoes in many ways the short story he would begin writing four months later (Smith 81). The dispatch tells of Hemingway's Swiss skiing adventure with a friend as they toss their skis into a "baggage car" and then board "a jerky little train" that takes them "straight up the side of the mountain on cogwheels" (*DLT* 421). After waxing their skis, the skiers head downhill "in one long, dropping, swooping, heart-plucking rush" (422), words that closely approximate those of the story: "The rush and the sudden swoop as he dropped down a steep undulation in the mountain side plucked Nick's mind out and left him only the wonderful flying, dropping sensation in his body" (*CSS* 143). But what makes the skiing of the dispatch vastly different from the skiing in the story is that its holiday slopes are crowded with a "long line of skiers," a "shooting stream of skiers," a "seemingly endless stream" (*DLT* 422–23). In the story, by contrast, no one else is there. George and Nick ski by themselves.

That Nick and George are alone on the slopes seems to me a crucial fact, but one that my students—and all other readings of the story I've found—seem to ignore. Since they will not have read the *Toronto Star Weekly* dispatch that implicitly contrasts crowded holiday slopes with the story's deserted terrain, I might ask the skiers in class how their own skiing experiences compare with that of Nick and George. I might ask, "Who else was there with you? Whom did you see?" Once we acknowledge that Nick and George are alone, the question then becomes, "Why? Why is no one else there?" Hemingway does not tell us, of course, any more than he directly states that the skiers are by themselves, but his chosen details allow us to infer an answer. Nick and George are alone on the slopes because adverse conditions make skiing difficult if not quite impossible. Not only is it "very cold" (*CSS* 147) but a powerful wind, a "gale," is "scouring" the hills where Nick and George have chosen to ski. What's more, the skiers are in the midst of a major snowstorm, "the snow driving like a sand-storm" (143), as they swoop down the mountainside. It is what Hemingway, looking back on a similar Swiss skiing expedition in January 1923, called a "Gawd awful storm and blizzard" (*SL* 84). Skiing conditions could not be much more dangerous and unpredictable. Unlike the accommodating "powder snow" (*DLT* 422) of "Christmas on the Roof of the World," the surface that Nick and

George encounter is a "wind-board crust" (*CSS* 143) which makes control difficult: Nick "slipped in a rush down the slope" the moment his skis touched the hard crust. At the top of the second slope Nick's "skis started slipping at the edge" (144), and he has no choice but to go down, down, down.

What then can we conclude with our students? That the severe cold and the powerful winds and the driving snow and the dangerous wind-board crust have deterred all would-be skiers—with the exception of Nick and George? I think so. Would Hemingway like us to see Nick and George's decision to ski despite blizzard conditions as a sign of their hardiness and courage and determination? Yes, I believe so. After all, it's their last chance—at least for a while and perhaps forever. George is returning to school that very evening, and Nick and Helen will soon enough be leaving Europe to become parents. Since "There isn't any good in promising" (*CSS* 147), Nick and George may never again be able to ski together. All the more reason to take advantage of what the present offers. Significantly, the first word of the story's final sentence is "Now."

If the story reflects Hemingway's view that life's limited opportunities must be seized—despite certain risks, despite probable pain, despite possible defeat—it also endorses an attitude of stoic acceptance. Nowhere in the story do we find either Nick or George lamenting the day's miserable weather or inhospitable slopes. Even when they are felled by soft snow that the wind had blown across their tracks, there is not a word of complaint, only brief recognition of the "lousy soft snow" before looking forward "over the khud" (143) to the next hill. Like the "specks of cork" that appear unbidden in your glass of wine, life's impurities and inevitable disappointments cannot be allowed to "matter," cannot be permitted to usurp life's pleasures and joys.

For Nick and George, as for Hemingway himself, there are few pleasures more intense and more exhilarating than the downhill run—"There's nothing really can touch skiing," Nick says; "It's too swell to talk about," George agrees (145). Before class begins I ask two students to prepare to read aloud to their classmates the description of George's skiing that constitutes the story's longest sentence:

> He looked up the hill. George was coming down in telemark position, kneeling; one leg forward and bent, the other trailing; his sticks hanging like some insect's thin legs, kicking up puffs of snow as they touched the surface and finally the whole kneeling, trailing figure coming around in a beautiful right curve, crouching, the legs shot forward and back, the body leaning out against the swing, the sticks accenting the curve like points of light, all in a wild cloud of snow. (144)

I want my students to hear the rhythms here, the series of participial phrases and absolutes that lead to the culminating "wild cloud of snow" so that they might imitate them in their next out-of-class writing assignment, which invites a more descriptive and narrative response:

> Write an informal, personal essay of 250 to 500 words in response to one (only one!) of these topics. If you like, try to write in Hemingway's style. Try to use some dialogue if you can. Like Hemingway, try to be specific and concrete. Try to create a scene. Try to show instead of just telling.
>
> 1. Downhill skiing "plucked Nick's mind out and left him only the wonderful, flying, dropping sensation in his body." Tell about a time when you became so excited and exhilarated by a physical activity that you, too, seemed to exist only in your body with your mind gone.
>
> 2. "Cross-County Snow" ends with Nick and George looking forward to their "run home together." Write about a time when you, too, were eagerly anticipating a meeting or an event.
>
> 3. Nick is now "glad" that Helen is pregnant although he hadn't been earlier. Write about a time when you changed your mind about a person or a happening.
>
> 4. Tell a story about a close friendship of yours—either a current or past one.
>
> 5. Nick and Helen do not want to return to the United States, but they will do so anyway. Write about a time when you had to do something you didn't want to do.
>
> 6. Write about a time when you were happy.

The central goal of all my courses is always the same: by the end of the term, I want my students to be more likely to read literature and to write by choice. All my assignments and other teaching strategies are designed to achieve this goal.

Notes

I am grateful to Ms. Kalinde Webb of Talawanda High School, Oxford, Ohio, for inviting me to her honors American literature classroom and to her student Benjamin C. Whiteman for granting me permission to print his written response to "Cross-Country Snow."

1. Hemingway encourages his readers to plumb the depths of his stories in this statement of his "ice-berg theory" from *Death in the Afternoon:* "If a writer of prose knows enough about what he is writing about he may omit things that he knows and the reader, if the writer is writing truly enough, will have a feeling of those things as strongly as though the writer had stated them. The dignity of movement of an ice-berg is due to only one-eighth of it being above water" (192).

2. I usually collect the written assignments at the start of class. Exceptions are if a student volunteers to read her/his writing aloud or if I begin class by forming students into groups of three or four to share their writing with classmates.

3. I collect, read quickly, and score these daily writing assignments, often without written comment of any kind, as check-plus (100 percent), check (80 percent), or check-minus (60 percent). My standards for these assignments are generous, so that scores—which count 10–15 percent of the course grade—usually raise semester averages. I return the scored daily assignments at the beginning of the following class. Several times during the semester I will ask a student to read aloud an especially insightful or provocative response. It's a lot of paperwork, especially with large classes, but I'm convinced that the writing—and my caring about it enough to collect and read it—helps students learn and grow.

4. In the story's earliest drafts the protagonist is named "Mike Adams," prompting some Hemingway scholars, including Smith, to conclude that George's addressing Nick as "Mike" is Hemingway's mistake. The story's evolution is an issue I would be more likely to take up in a graduate course.

5. See Daiker below.

6. That Hemingway recognized the difference is clear from *A Moveable Feast:* "There were no ski lifts from Shruns and no funiculars" (196).

Works Cited

American Heritage Dictionary. Houghton Mifflin, 1985.

Baker, Carlos. *Hemingway: A Life Story.* Scribner, 1969.

Bloom, Harold, ed. *Ernest Hemingway's* The Sun Also Rises. Infobase Publishing, 2011, pp. 165–78.

Daiker, Donald A. "Jake Barnes as Teacher and Learner: The Pedagogy of *The Sun Also Rises.*" *Hemingway Review,* vol. 27, no. 1, Fall 2007, 74–88.

Hemingway, Ernest. *The Complete Short Stories of Ernest Hemingway: The Finca Vigía Edition.* Scribner, 1987.

———. *Dateline Toronto: The Complete* Toronto Star *Dispatches, 1920–1924,* edited by William White. Scribner, 1985.

———. *Death in the Afternoon.* Scribner, 1932.

———. *Green Hills of Africa.* Scribner, 1935.

———. *In Our Time.* Scribner, 1953.

———. *A Moveable Feast.* Scribner, 1964.

———. *Selected Letters, 1917–1961,* edited by Carlos Baker, Scribner, 1981.

———. *The Sun Also Rises.* Scribner, 1954.

Murray, Donald M. *Write to Learn.* Cengage Learning, 2004.

Reynolds, Michael. *Hemingway: The Paris Years.* Norton, 1989.

Smith, Paul. *A Reader's Guide to the Short Stories of Ernest Hemingway.* G. K. Hall, 1989.

The Things That Nick Adams Carried
to the Big Two-Hearted River

Frederic J. Svoboda

First, let me explain some of the contexts for my teaching of Hemingway's classic long-short story "Big Two-Hearted River." This story of a Great War veteran fishing in Michigan's Upper Peninsula (UP) is presented in two sections covering two days and is the conclusion to Hemingway's 1925 short story collection *In Our Time.* The story encapsulates most of the previous experiences of Nick Adams, Hemingway's alter ego and protagonist of many of the collection's stories.

As it happens, almost all my teaching of this story (and of Hemingway's others works) has taken place in Michigan institutions of higher education, first at Michigan State University as grad student, instructor, and visiting assistant professor, and now as a professor at the University of Michigan–Flint, a largely commuter student branch of the university. This is significant. In discussing literature, we tend not to say a lot about our students, although in fact good teachers almost always do a great deal to accommodate their particular audiences.

Unlike the students of someone like Judy Henn, whose teaching career was spent largely in Israel, my students may not have to work very hard to imagine the settings of Hemingway's Michigan stories. Mine can fairly easily drive to the settings of the Nick Adams stories, and a number have done so. The Walloon Lake/Petoskey area setting of many early stories is maybe three and a half hours away from Flint by automobile. Seney, setting of "Big Two-Hearted River," is five to six hours away. In the Motor State, such distances are negligible. Michiganians routinely drive such distances for weekend getaways, much less for longer vacations.

To understand "Big Two-Hearted River," it is useful to understand the differences between Michigan's Lower and Upper Peninsulas.

The concept "Up North" is a recognized trope among Michigan natives. "Up North" connotes a weekend or a getaway of several weeks to the cottaging areas of the very civilized northern Lower Michigan, the peninsula bounded by Lake Huron on the east and Lake Michigan on the west. (The Hemingways most often traveled to Petoskey and nearby Walloon Lake via Lake Michigan steamship from the port of Chicago.) Now, as then, this part of Michigan is eminently civilized, what I elsewhere have called "a false wilderness," where one can pretend to confront wilderness while enjoying almost all the civilized comforts of home. As did the Hemingways, some vacationers still manage to spend much of the summer Up North in a season that begins with the week of July 4.

The Upper Peninsula connotes a "wilder," more natural experience, a little harder to reach for a weekend even today, impossible to reach quickly when Hemingway was young, and this is reflected in "Big Two-Hearted River." The UP is bounded on the south by Lakes Huron and Michigan, and on the north by Lake Superior. Now reachable from the Lower Peninsula of Michigan via the four-lane Mackinac Bridge, the UP in Hemingway's time was accessible only via railroad car ferry, further enforcing the region's isolation.

But not all students, even in Michigan, are familiar with Up North. Or they are familiar in different ways. The family-oriented, genteel cottaging experience of Michigan is generally very different from the fishing and hunting experience of Michigan. The latter is mostly still an experience of men and more likely to take place in rustic state forest campgrounds or just in random locations in state forests, the remnants of the logged-over Michigan of the nineteenth century in which Hemingway similarly camped during his teens.

Hemingway's experiences (and stories) bridge these two different Up North experiences with the contrast seen most clearly in "The Doctor and the Doctor's Wife," where a hunter husband and genteel wife clash because of their different perceptions of the state. Now as then, many of those who go Up North don't have particularly grueling outdoor experiences. They instead spend time at beaches, on speedboats, or walking the downtowns of Petoskey, Charlevoix, and Traverse City, shopping heavens on greater and lesser scale.

Class differences intrude in students' perceptions of the stories, also. Unlike Michigan State or the University of Michigan–Ann Arbor, the University of Michigan–Flint (UMF) has largely a working-class student body. Hunting and fishing tend somewhat to skew working class, as do camping in state park and state forest campgrounds, riding off-road vehicles in summer and snowmobiles in winter.

Cottaging tends to be solidly middle if not upper middle class. Cottages are expensive, particularly lakefront cottages like the Hemingways' Windemere. (There also is an upper-class northern experience, represented by upscale Bay Harbor, Harbor Springs, and Mackinac Island after 5:00 P.M. when the day-trippers go home.)

This is all to make the point that there is no single Up North experience in our time; nor was there in Hemingway's time. There also is another: experience of war and the military, which feeds into the students' perceptions of "Big Two-Hearted River." When I first taught the novel, I taught some World War II and Korean War vets, but mostly Vietnam War vets. Now I still see a few vets of the Gulf War, but more veterans of Iraq and Afghanistan. Since UMF has students predominantly from working-class families, many are frontline veterans (most still men, though a few women). More will be attending the school in the future. This is further to make the point that there is no unitary point of view on Hemingway and "Big Two-Hearted River," even among Michigan students.

Now to teaching the story.

This essay is called "The Things That Nick Adams Carried to the Big Two-Hearted River" partly as a tip of the hat to Tim O'Brien's excellent Vietnam War unified short story collection, *The Things They Carried* (1990). O'Brien lists the physical things that his soldiers carried into battle (as Hemingway lists the things that Nick carries in his backpack), but O'Brien also gets at the emotional burdens that they bear, and Nick's emotional burdens are a huge part of the subtext of "Big Two-Hearted River." There is no doubt that O'Brien was a reader of Hemingway and understood the metaphorical uses of physical burdens to a writer of psychologically evocative fiction.

This essay also is so named because of a technique I have used to bridge the gaps between the many different experiences of the Michigan north that my students bring to the novel. It began at Michigan State when I still was in graduate school, years before O'Brien's novel was published.

Hemingway was not much in vogue then in the early 1970s. Some students understood him immediately and intuitively. Young men with experiences of the outdoors or of war often could discuss "Big Two-Hearted River" with an insight that they could not bring to most other works of literature. (They knew the subject matter and its resonance in their own lives so well that they did not need to be able to follow the ins and outs of Hemingway's subtle literary technique.)

Other students seemed not to understand him at all, indeed to resist understanding him, as if there were a bad old Hemingway who reeked of machismo
and a lack of sympathy for female characters. (I think that we now know that
this Hemingway was much a fictional creation, partly of the author, partly of
his publisher and publicists, and partly of those critics who wanted him to be a
sure, straight guide to a simple life rather than a chronicler of life's ambiguities.)

Let me tell you a story. One day something occurred in a class I was teaching
as a TA, a 400-level modern American literature course. We were talking about
"Big Two-Hearted River," and one student obviously *had just had enough!* I'm
sure you have had the experience, either of one of your students who is mad as
hell and just can't take it anymore, or perhaps your personal experience of having been that student. That this student wasn't being taught by kindly old Virgil
Scott as intended and had me as a last-minute substitution might have been a
part of the student's problem. In any case, she had been seething for much of
the class period, she had had it, and she finally let loose. What she said, more
or less, was, "I just can't stand this story. I don't care about the main character,
I don't care why he is wandering around the Upper Peninsula by himself, and
besides, I just don't believe the story. Look at all the stuff Hemingway says he
is carrying! No one could cart all that stuff around!"

I took a look at her, and not to be unkind, she looked like a person who
never had been off a sidewalk in her life. But I didn't say anything about that.
Instead, in one of my few instances of recognizing that the famous "teachable
moment" was at hand, I looked at the clock, saw that there were only a few
minutes left in the class period, and punted: "We're out of time. Let's all think
about the stuff that Nick Adams is carrying in his backpack, and we'll start our
discussion next time with that. Class dismissed, and thank you for bringing
this up, Michelle."

I knew that I had her, with only a little preparation required for the next
class period. I was in my backpacking phase at that point in my life, and as
soon as I got home I started listing all the things that Hemingway had Nick
carrying, weighing and estimating weights, and throwing things into my oldest canvas backpack. I had to go out to buy a few items, mostly canned food,
and I couldn't find a canvas bucket at short notice, but for the most part I was
able to recreate Nick's load with a fair amount of accuracy.

Just for your edification, here's my list with estimated weights:

Items in Backpack	Pounds	Ounces
Duluth canoe pack with tumpline	5	
brown canvas tent (tarp)	5	
rope		8
leather thong		1
cheesecloth for mosquito net		8
three blankets	6	
camp ax	3	8
pocketknife		3
paper sack of nails		10
can of pork and beans	1	
can of spaghetti	1	8
can of apricots	1	
can of condensed milk	1	
jar of ketchup	1	
jar of apple butter	1	
loaf of bread		12
large onion	1	
buckwheat pancake flour	2	
Crisco or similar grease in can	1	
wire grill		10
frying pan	2	8
tin cup		6
tin plate		5
spoon		2
oiled (waxed) paper		8
canvas bucket	1	4
coffee pot and coffee	1	
matches		2
empty milk bottle		6
leather rod-case and fly rod	3	
fly reel		10

aluminum leader box/gut leaders		8
fish hooks and flies in fly book		4
flour sack	1	
landing net	1	8
cigarettes		4
map		4

maybe:

.22 Colt Woodsman pistol	2	10
Kodak camera	1	
(A friend of Hemingway had these two items on a previous trip.)		
Pack Weight	55	12

(Plus additional clothing and food)

Nick's Clothing

wool socks
boots (called "shoes" interchangeably, though Nick might have a pair of canvas shoes for wading as well as hiking boots)
pants
hat
khaki shirt with two pockets
Minimal Clothing Weight: 7–10 lbs.
Total Weight Carried, at least 62–65 lbs.

I showed up at the next class session wearing a khaki shirt with two breast pockets to echo Nick's androgynous military shirt, hiking boots and the like, and toting my backpack, which I then proceeded to unload in front of the class, discussing all the things as they came out of the pack.

I don't always bring the pack when I discuss this presentation today. I'm older now, and besides, I can't imagine the airline baggage overcharges, much less explaining the camp ax and pistol to Homeland Security. However, I have done the presentation complete with props at several Michigan Hemingway Society weekends in Petoskey.

And there are several serious points to be made.

You can carry what Nick Adams carried. In the modern era of lightweight camping you probably would not choose to do so, but you can. (As Nick says to himself, "[You've] got a right to eat this kind of stuff, if [you're] willing to carry it" [*IOT* 187]).

Not everyone has the same experience of the world. Certainly Michelle did not, but even she had to admit that there was something to be said for being open to these other experiences, and trusting your author to convey them to you with some accuracy. (Of course, the wackiness of one's instructor showing up in full pack mule mode made the presentation worthwhile just from the point of view of entertainment.)

Michelle also gave me points for taking her complaint seriously, something that we all need to remember to do as teachers: to remember how much specialized knowledge we carry that is not immediately apparent to many undergraduates. I didn't make fun of her, but I did show her what might have been possible for Nick as backpacker and post-traumatic stress disorder (PTSD) sufferer.

I also made points with the hunting and fishing guys in the course for taking seriously something—the weight Nick carried—that they probably already had figured out for themselves. Incidentally, discussing the accuracy of my weight estimates sometimes can become a major topic in itself.

Perhaps a more serious point: sometimes realistic presentation also becomes metaphor, in several ways.

First, Nick's load begins to approximate the loads that World War I infantrymen carried into combat, at least until the last year of the war when the need for mobility began to trump carrying everything that an infantryman might possibly need to consolidate a static position. Most authorities put that weight earlier in the war at sixty pounds and up.[1] Some of my students over the years have known about infantry combat loads from firsthand experience; if anything, these have increased considerably in recent years. Some of the members of that particular course tried toting the pack after class. (It took quite a while to repack it all.) That got them a direct access to the "reality" behind the story.

Second, Nick is carrying some emotional or psychological burdens as well as his physical burdens. This is not just a story about fishing, but also about PTSD (which had not been so named when I first did my backpack presentation, but about which Hemingway was an expert, courtesy of his being wounded on the Italian Front and its aftermath). If Hemingway is not going to discuss these burdens directly—as he chose to do when he omitted the "On Writing" section of "Big Two-Hearted River" presenting Nick as a writer—he has to hint at them somehow.

I could go on, but I hope that I have suggested here something of the ways in which one can't assume that even students close in space or time to the setting of a story will comprehend that setting completely. I hope I have suggested that there is a variety of experiences that students bring to a story such as "Big Two-Hearted River," and that we have to respect and respond to those differences, whether students know a lot or almost nothing. I hope that I also have suggested that Hemingway took as careful account of the surfaces of his stories as their deeper implications, even to weighing the physical burdens that his protagonist carried.

I hope that's enough.

Note

1. The most detailed discussion of this I have found including weight estimates for the major combatants, lists of items, and photos is in Ellis, *Eye-Deep in Hell*, 32–37.

Works Cited

Ellis, John. *Eye-Deep in Hell: Trench Warfare in World War I.* Johns Hopkins UP, 1973.
Hemingway, Ernest. *In Our Time.* Scribner, 1930.
O'Brien, Tim. *The Things They Carried.* Houghton Mifflin, 1990.

"Doesn't It Mean Anything to You?"
Teaching "Hills Like White Elephants"

Marc Seals

Ernest Hemingway's "Hills Like White Elephants" surely serves as one of the most reliable workhorses in the college English classroom. The story's short length—under 1,500 words, a mere four pages in the Finca Vigía edition of *The Complete Short Stories of Ernest Hemingway*—makes it useful for a number of pedagogical reasons. First, the story provides a concise introduction to Ernest Hemingway's fiction and narrative techniques. Second, "Hills Like White Elephants" provides an ideal subject for introducing students to academic research and the use of electronic databases. Third, the story may be used to introduce the writing processes of literary analysis. In short, the reading and discussion of "Hills Like White Elephants" provides an introduction into everything that I do and want students to do in the undergraduate classroom.

I use "Hills Like White Elephants" in my first-year composition classroom before even beginning the first writing project—or, rather, "Hills Like White Elephants" introduces the first writing project, which is a literary analysis essay. In an era of standardized tests, many students say they've never written such an essay. Rather than bore the better-prepared students while tutoring the other students, I model academic discussion, research, and analysis using "Hills Like White Elephants"; this approach holds the interest of those who already know how to write literary analysis while introducing these skills to the others. I allot three class periods for this introductory lesson (which I think would also be useful in the high school classroom).

On the first day (Monday), I begin with a discussion of Ernest Hemingway. I ask the students what they know—or what they think they know—about

Hemingway. I receive the usual misconceptions, oversimplifications, and faulty assumptions, and then I attempt to correct the record. We very briefly outline his life, discussing his family, the trauma of World War I, his marriages, his writing career, his hobbies, and his death. Students are always astounded by Hemingway's life, and someone often remarks that he sounds (and looks) like "the most interesting man in the world" from the *Dos Equis* beer advertisements. This discussion grabs the students' interest, as well as proving useful during the subsequent discussions of "Hills Like White Elephants." We then discuss "the Hemingway style," and I explain Hemingway's iceberg principle. I read the relevant quote from Hemingway's *Death in the Afternoon:* "If a writer of prose knows enough of what he is writing about he may omit things that he knows and the reader, if the writer is writing truly enough, will have a feeling of those things as strongly as though the writer had stated them. The dignity of movement of an ice-berg is due to only one-eighth of it being above water. A writer who omits things because he does not know them only makes hollow places in his writing" (192). I remind them what they learned in middle school language arts class about plot. They recite the elements for Freytag's pyramid together (at least to a point): exposition, rising action, climax, falling action, and resolution (or dénouement, if the students are showing off). I ask the class, "What if an author only gives the reader a fragment of this? Is it still a story?"

The class is then ready to read "Hills Like White Elephants." I ask if anyone has read the story previously, and there are usually a few students who read it in high school. I instruct these students not to give anything away about the story. I hand out copies of the story and read it aloud to the class, which takes about eight minutes. After reading, I allow a long silence before asking, Who has no idea what to make of the story? Most students raise their hands, and they are visibly relieved to see that they are not alone in their confusion. This confusion is one of the main advantages of the story. Most students, regardless of their level of literary acuity, are in a similar state of confusion; thus, students must delve more deeply into this deceptively simple story. I ask the class to tell me what's going on in "Hills Like White Elephants." Students will volunteer the surface details—there is a couple waiting for a train in Spain, and they are arguing. I ask the class, "What is the subject of their argument?" Another long silence usually follows. If a student ventures, "An abortion?" I ask that student to point to the evidence in the story (for the benefit of the other students who usually bear expressions of utter disbelief). If no student has picked up on these clues, I ask the class to look at what the couple *does* say about the unspoken subject. Students will invariably point to the evidence (the mention of the simple operation that's not really an operation, the phrase "just let the air in," the fact that the man does not "want anyone else," etc.), and a student will invariably blurt out the topic of the argument. When this finally happens, I am quick to point out that this is not the "answer" to the story, that "Hills Like White Elephants" is far more than a fictive riddle to be solved with a one-word answer. Paul Cioe correctly argues that "the story is about the way the characters communicate (or don't communicate) about the question (or and question) as much as it is about the question itself" (103).

I ask the class what questions they have about the story (and they have many), and we discuss the answers. Why is Jig drinking if she is pregnant? (The idea that pregnant women should not drink is surprisingly recent.) Is the couple married? (Probably not.) Why does the reader know Jig's name, but not that of "the man"? (The story is told with a third-person objective narration.) What is their age difference? (Hmmm. . .) Who "wins" the argument? (Good question.) We discuss these questions, and I attempt to get the students to answer (providing evidence from the text to support these answers). The best instance of this strategy came last year when a student asked why the man in the story is never named. Another student excitedly pointed out that the reader knows Jig's name because it is in the dialogue of the story. This knowledge (and lack of knowledge) reduces the reader into the role of mere objective observer, the student continued; might his objective narrative stance stem from Hemingway's experience as a newspaper writer? (To be honest, I was as stunned as the rest of the class at this student's insight and his skill in expressing such insight.) I ask them how long the story takes—they look at the opening paragraph and note that the story covers about forty minutes. I point out that it took only eight minutes to read aloud and three of those minutes were narration. That means that there is more than half an hour of silence between the man and Jig, and that silence has probably been excruciating for them both. (It would be a curious bit of performance art to read the story with all of the silence intact, but I fear that I would lose the class.) This discussion and question-and-answer brainstorming closes the first day and begins the second.

Many students have deeper insight on the second day (Wednesday), perhaps indicating that they have been thinking about the story. I ask the class if anyone has done any research, and a few students always raise their hands. When I ask what research strategies were used, I usually get a sheepish grin and a meek confession of "Google" or "Wikipedia." This provides the opening for introducing the electronic databases available through the library's website. Though Phillip Sipiora observed in his 1984 article about the story that "Hills

Like White Elephants" "has received scant critical attention" (50), the same cannot be said any longer. Before using a specific database, I first bring up the campus's library website on the classroom projector. We begin with what seems like the easiest option—a simultaneous search of all databases. Students soon see that this returns many results, but that many of these results are not academic sources or are repeat hits. Then I show them that they can sort the databases by subject, and that by choosing "English/Literature" they may select databases that only have scholarly (and relevant) sources. I demonstrate that the MLA database has 65 sources—63 of those in English and 16 of those are available in full text. I tell them that we'll return to these on Friday.

We spend the rest of class discussing and researching the meaning of the title—the real focus of our mock essay. I ask them why they think the story is called "Hills Like White Elephants." After a few minutes of brainstorming, we have generated a list on the board—the idea that elephants never forget and the idiom "the elephant in the room" are two common theories that arise. Eventually, I ask them why *white* elephants. Someone usually asks if it has anything to do with a white elephant gift exchange. I ask that student to explain to the class what this event is, and they say something along the lines of "It's when people bring a present that they don't want and there's a game redistributing the presents." I say, "So it's about a gift that one person doesn't want and another person does." This usually elicits an audible "Oooh" as they make the obvious connection to the story. I ask them if they know the roots of the popular concept of white elephant gift exchanges and white elephant sales. No student has ever known the answer. I explain that it is rooted in Buddhist legend. According to *The Life of Buddha,* by André-Ferdinand Hérold:[1]

> The same hour that spring was born, a dream came to Maya as she slept. She saw a young elephant descending from the sky. [. . .] it was as white as the snow on mountain-tops. Maya saw it enter her womb, and thousands of Gods suddenly appeared before her. They praised her with immortal songs, and Maya understood that nevermore would she know disquietude or hatred or anger. Then she awoke. She was happy; it was a happiness she had never felt before. [. . .] The queen told [the king] of the dream she had had; then added: "My lord, there are brahmans who are clever at interpreting dreams. Send for them. [. . .]" The king agreed, and brahmans [. . .] were summoned to the palace. When they had heard Maya's story they spoke [. . .]: "A great joy is to be yours, O king, O queen. A son will be born to you, distinguished by the favor of the Gods. [. . .] O master, O mistress, your son will be a Buddha!" (8–10)

As a result of this legend, white elephants are symbols of power, fertility, and divine blessing, sacred in the Buddhist world and not to be used for labor. If a ruler wished to bring down an ambitious person, he could give him a white elephant as a gift. The resulting drain on this person's resources might be his financial ruin. Thus, a white elephant is a gift that might be seen as both a great blessing and a great burden. This usually elicits another "Oooh!" from the class—they immediately see that this might apply to the story.

We return to the results of our database search and look at the keywords to see if any might reflect this interpretation. I point out that they could skim these articles in a few hours, but to save time, I pull up several that are especially relevant—those by Nilofer Hashmi, Kenneth Johnston, Lewis Weeks, and Hilary Justice. I spend some time with the class reading relevant quotes from each of the aforementioned articles. The Hashmi article summarizes many interpretations of the title:

> The title […] has particularly fascinated scholars, in terms of its imperviousness to obvious interpretation on the one hand, and of the importance given to it by Hemingway on the other. Critics have found themselves searching in various directions for an "explanation," including the suggestive appearance and color of the hills (Abdoo 238), the connotation of an unwanted gift implied in the term "white elephant" (Kozikowski 107), and the contradictory implications of "an annoyingly useless gift" and "a possession of great value" (DeFalco 169). (74–75)

This quote helps introduce the subject of the story's title as a concern of various critics, and Nashmi's use of quotes from other critics allows me to demonstrate the key concept that good academic writing is a conversation (between the author, the reader, and the critics of the past). The Johnston article analyzes (among other things) the use of the setting to reflect the couple's dilemma: "The description of the Ebro valley embodies the poles of the conflict too: It is both barren and fruitful. On the side which they sit facing, there are no trees and no shade, and in the distance the country is brown and dry; on the other side of the valley, there are 'fields of grain and trees along the banks of the Ebro'" (235). Weeks addresses the applicability of the phrase "white elephant," writing, "Our immediate understanding of the white elephant reference […] is probably that associated with the ubiquitous white elephant sale. […] To the man, the child is a white elephant that, in his selfishness, he wants to get rid of. To the girl, the child is a white elephant only insofar as its father rejects it; she would like to bear the child" (76). Justice discusses the "omission of the word 'abortion'" (18). I ask the class, "What's that phrase for an uncomfortable topic that no one wants to say aloud?"; someone always smiles wryly and says, "The elephant in the room" (eliciting a third "Oooh" from the class). Justice also addresses the meaning of the phrase "white elephants," explaining, "To begin with the title, a first connotation of 'white elephants' is purely American: unwanted junk. [. . .] The second, historical layer of meaning embraces both aspects: 'white elephants' as a gift bringing both honor and ruin to its recipient. At first glance, it means one thing. At second, it means two—not one of two, but one and two. Honor and ruin" (18). Finally, Justice analyzes the symbolism of the setting:

> The valley setting is neatly bisected into two sides, "this" side (the infertile side, "brown and dry" with "no trees"), and "the other" side (the fertile side: fields of grain, the river, the trees), by not one but "two lines of rails," between which the couple sits "at a table in the shade'" (CSS 211). The setting is introduced in two stages. In the opening paragraph, we are given the bleak view; in the second, a "lovely" view (213). At first glance, the valley is one way: barren. Later, we learn that it is two: both barren and fertile, simultaneously. (18)

I then point out to the class that Justice, like any good literary critic, backs up her argument with quotes from the story—and they should do the same in their literary analysis essays. Several of these articles are not available in full-text through the database, so I have the opportunity to demonstrate how to submit an interlibrary loan request—an important research skill that is likely unfamiliar to new college students.

We set out to outline a mock essay on day three (Friday). I point out that the idea of meaning of the title in "Hills" is merely a topic—not a thesis—so we craft a thesis together. I try to make the students do the heavy lifting here; one could conduct this as a class, or the instructor could have the students break into small groups. In the end, our goal is to have a thesis, several main points that support this thesis, direct quotes or examples from the story for each of these points, and a critical quote or two to support each the points. A typical example of an informal essay is included below. Since I've already quoted the relevant passages, I will not do so again here.

Topic: the significance of the title "Hills Like White Elephants"

Thesis: In Ernest Hemingway's 1927 story "Hills Like White Elephants," the author establishes a clear parallel between the title and the dilemma facing the couple.

Point 1: "the elephant in the room" as relevant idiom
    Textual support: the fact that the words "abortion," "baby," or "pregnancy" never appear in the story
    Critical support: Hilary Justice's discussion of the omission
Point 2: analysis of the setting
    Textual support: quotes from the story about the simultaneously barren and fertile valley
    Critical support: relevant quotes from Kenneth Johnston and Hilary Justice
Point 3: "white elephant" as relevant idiom
    Textual support: "white elephants" mentioned four times in the story
    Critical support: relevant quotes from André-Ferdinand Hérold, Lewis Weeks, and Hilary Justice

I am not attempting to teach formal outlining; if this is a priority in your classroom, then obviously the outline can be adapted. Once we have the outline projected on the screen, I ask if writing all this into an essay would be difficult. Someone inevitably says, "No, the hard work is already done—all I'd have to do is put it all in sentence form with transitions and such." I smile and say, "You mean that if you've read carefully, thought deeply, researched well, and planned logically (a task that took a few hours here), the essay writes itself?" That's pretty much it. They are fully prepared to tackle this task on their own (with guidance, of course).

Several students have been so taken with Hemingway's style that they've asked for suggestions for further reading; I usually tell them to start with the Nick Adams stories. Such was the personal meaning of the story for one young woman that she came to class later in the semester showing off her "white elephant" tattoo—though that may have revealed more about her history than the class needed to know. More importantly, the literary analysis essays that follow (on a different story) are much better than the ones I received before modeling the strategies with "Hills Like White Elephants."

Note

1. Though this is a rather old book (1927), the details of this tale do not differ materially from other more modern translations (such as Mitchell's *The Buddha*, 12–15). I use the Hérold text here merely because it is available online and it is more concise with regards to this account.

Works Cited and Consulted

Cioe, Paul. "Teaching Hemingway's 'Hills Like White Elephants': A Simple Operation?" *Eureka Studies in Teaching Short Fiction,* vol. 3, no. 1, 2002, pp. 101–5.

Hashmi, Nilofer. "'Hills Like White Elephants': The Jilting of Jig." *Hemingway Review,* vol. 23, no. 1, 2003, pp. 72–83.

Hemingway, Ernest. *Death in the Afternoon.* Scribner, 1932.

———. "Hills Like White Elephants." *The Complete Short Stories of Ernest Hemingway: The Finca Vigía Edition.* Scribner, 1987.

Hérold, André-Ferdinand. *The Life of Buddha.* Boni, 1927.

Johnston, Kenneth G. "'Hills Like White Elephants': Lean, Vintage Hemingway." *Studies in American Fiction,* vol. 10, no. 2, 1982, 233–38.

Justice, Hilary K. "'Well, Well, Well': Cross-Gendered Autobiography and the Manuscript of "Hills Like White Elephants." *Hemingway Review,* vol. 18, no. 1, 1998, pp. 17–32.

Mitchell, Robert Allen. *The Buddha: His Life Revisited.* New York, 1991.

Sipiora, Phillip. "Hemingway's 'Hills Like White Elephants.'" *Explicator,* vol. 42, no. 3, 1984, p. 50.

Smith, Paul. *A Reader's Guide to the Short Stories of Ernest Hemingway.* G. K. Hall, 1989.

Weeks, Lewis E. "Hemingway Hills: Symbolism in 'Hills Like White Elephants.'" *Studies in Short Fiction,* vol. 17, 1980, pp. 75–77.

Listening between the Lines

"Hills Like White Elephants" and "A Clean, Well-Lighted Place"

Verna Kale

Ernest Hemingway's iceberg theory is well known to those who teach and study his work, even those who haven't made it through all four hundred plus pages of *Death in the Afternoon,* the treatise on bullfighting (and writing) in which Hemingway originates the metaphor (192). We may try to impart the author's theory of omission to our students in lecture and class discussion, but if students are not particularly careful readers, or if they are suspicious of "reading too much into" a text, they may prove resistant to the idea. As any English teacher can attest, there is no purgatory like the "discussion" that occurs when students have not done the day's assigned reading.

In this essay I provide lesson plans for teaching Ernest Hemingway's short stories "Hills Like White Elephants" and "A Clean, Well-Lighted Place." These lesson plans require students to read the stories out loud so they can note, in real time, the length of the pauses in conversation, and identify, precisely, who in each story says what. The students are thus impelled to consider essential problems that they encounter in the texts—cruxes they would otherwise have missed had they simply allowed their eyes to run quickly over each page as they raced to complete their homework. Not only does this performance of the text ensure that all students do the reading—and read critically—it also provides an "amusing yet instructive" method of accommodating a variety of learning styles (Hemingway, *Death* 133).[1]

A significant number of today's college students are underprepared for the traditional readings and discussion-based model of college English instruction. The National Center for Education Statistics reports that in 2015 (the last year for which data is available for twelfth graders) only 37 percent of students were reading "at or above Proficient"; meanwhile the US Bureau of Labor Statistics reports that 66.7 percent of 2017 high school graduates ages sixteen to twenty-four enrolled in colleges or universities. Whether or not these students "should" be in college—the necessity of a four-year degree for all is another discussion—does not change the fact that they are enrolling, alongside their better-prepared peers, in literature courses that satisfy core, elective, and major requirements. Instructors must create assignments that benefit these lagging students while still challenging the students who are "proficient" or "advanced" and ready for the rigorous work of literary analysis.

The in-class activities I outline below encourage students to move beyond the basics of plot summary and to generate readings based on textual evidence. This kind of collaborative learning—working in groups toward a common goal—requires problem solving, teamwork, and analysis. The lesson is also inclusive, allowing reluctant readers to build reading comprehension while students with more advanced critical thinking skills work on close reading. Though I discuss two stories in particular, the essential idea—that performing Hemingway stories in class reveals the underside of the iceberg—works with other stories as well.[2]

Hills Like White Elephants

"Hills Like White Elephants" (1927) is one of Hemingway's most widely anthologized short stories. Students who encountered the story in their high school English courses, and many of the better readers, come to class already aware that the "awfully simple operation" the couple argues about is an abortion (212). Instead of working toward this conclusion in class discussion, I start with it—or rather, the students start with it before I get the chance. Eager to be the first to reveal the "spoiler," students race each other to inform their classmates, a revelation that often takes the other students by surprise. More than ninety years after the story was published in the little magazine *transition* and in the collection *Men without Women* (1927), the topic of abortion is still taboo enough that students who did not do the reading or who found the story confusing begin to look more alert. We may spend a few minutes demonstrating to the unconvinced that, indeed, an abortion is part of the submerged seven-eighths of this particular iceberg, but typically students are eager to move on to (what they now believe to be) the essential question: does the girl go through with it?

Trying to figure out what Jig decides by story's end is a useful exercise in close reading that can be teased out over an entire class period (or more). Today's students, who have likely never seen a beer bottle without a surgeon general's warning on it, tend to obsess over the amount of alcohol Jig drinks in the story. Some are not easily dissuaded from the opinion that this recklessness clearly indicates her intention to abort, but this red herring can nevertheless serve as a jumping-off point for examining other details in the story more closely.[3] The goal of the ensuing discussion is not to reach a consensus but to practice close reading habits: making an argument and supporting that argument with analysis of the available evidence.

Does Jig abort? Does the couple stay together? The story teaches well precisely because there is no identifiably "right" answer to these questions: over the years scholars have argued persuasively for any number of interpretations. Initially, they were in general agreement that Jig goes through with the abortion. Elizabeth A. Flynn describes "Hills Like White Elephants" as a story of "female vulnerability and defeat" (244) and Stephen R. Portch speaks for an imagined readership that "finish[es] the story despising the man and sympathizing with the woman" (45). At least one scholar (Hannum) concludes that Jig has the abortion but leaves the man. Determined to know the unknowable, scholars have looked to the minutest details of the story for answers, publishing articles in *Explicator* on everything from the beaded curtain (Gilmour) to calculations of the couple's blood alcohol content (Abdoo). It has even been argued that the girl has the abortion in hopes of saving the relationship only to be jilted by the man afterward (Hashmi).

Stanley Renner was among the first to suggest that the girl decides against having the abortion and suggests, too, that the man, reluctantly, goes along with her wishes. Hilary K. Justice expands upon Renner's reading with additional support drawn from manuscript evidence and Hemingway's biography. As Justice notes, however, in the absence of the archival material—which was unavailable to any reader in Hemingway's day and is likewise beyond the immediate grasp of the student reading the story right before class—the story's conclusion remains utterly ambiguous. Not only can one argue quite persuasively for any and all of these conclusions, the story—with its railroad station nestled between two sets of mountains—is itself built to suggest a binary, "both spatial and rhetorical" (Justice, "Well" 25).

Debating what happens in the story is a useful if ultimately doomed exercise, and instructors may wish to allow class discussion to continue organically as long as the students' attention spans allow. As Meg Gillette rightly notes, "Ultimately, though, it's the reader, and not the characters, who supplies the literary performance the story desires. With her exhortation, 'Would you please please please please please please please stop talking?,' Jig concedes the failure of their language to produce an accord" (57). Likewise, the language of criticism (and class discussion) will—and should—fail to produce an accord. If a class does manage to reach a consensus, the instructor might well step in to offer one of the alternative points of view cited here. More important than reaching consensus is reaching the (to students, less satisfying) understanding that this story, which Hemingway himself recognized as "hard," is about a failure to communicate.[4]

Students, perhaps to their credit, tend to jump too quickly to defend Jig against the man and in so doing fail to note the tension and ambivalence that runs through the story (and that drives the still-ongoing critical debate). In reading the story out loud, and—this part is essential—acting out the motions described in the narration, the awkward pauses in the story overtake the classroom.[5] In this case, awkward pauses produce class discussion rather than stymie it.

The classroom should be set up so that there is a table with two chairs (or two desks pushed together) to represent the table at which much of the dialogue takes place and another table or desk to serve as the bar. Plastic cups can represent the beer and the anisette and assist the students in visualizing the amount of time spent silently drinking—and the amount of alcohol consumed. The instructor begins the read-through by assigning parts (or taking volunteers): the man, Jig, and the server. The instructor should read the longer passages of exposition and serve as a sort of director, providing guidance (as needed) on when and how long to be silent and where to move, as indicated by the text.

Thirty-five minutes elapse from the beginning of the story ("the express from Barcelona would come in forty minutes" [211]) to the end ("The train comes in five minutes" [214]). The rest of the dialogue takes up about five minutes total. One of the enticing ambiguities of the story is figuring out how the other thirty minutes are spent. There is no definitive answer, but the instructor should make sure that a realistic amount of time is used up by the server preparing the drinks at the "bar" and by the man and girl drinking at the table. When prepping for class, the instructor should do a few (timed) run-throughs themselves to figure out where to suggest introducing these pauses, as they are not always clearly indicated in the text.

Does the couple finish the beers before ordering the Anis del Toro? If so, the student-actors should sit, silently finishing the "drink," for a few minutes between the girl's first remark about the white elephants and her question about the beaded curtain. Perhaps they order the anisette before the beers are finished, in which case even longer pauses must be added elsewhere in the story. In either case, the instructor should be sure that the server returns to the bar and acts out the motion of pouring the liquor and the water between the otherwise seamless dialogue in which the man places the order—"Yes, with water"—and the girl tastes the resulting drink—"It tastes like licorice" (212).

In addition to directing students' attention to these textually prescribed pauses, the instructor might also note where other, unsignified, long periods of silence likely occur, though ideally students will be given the opportunity to decide the locations of these lacunae for themselves. For example, there is probably a pause where "The girl looked across at the hills" (212). The silence should last long enough for the couple to finish the anisette and whatever remains of their beers, because the man then asks, "Should we have another drink?" (212). Students may elect to pause here for the server to silently bring two more beers before the man remarks that they are "nice and cool" (212). However, the story is yet again maddeningly unspecific: it is possible the girl never finishes the drink and that the beers described here as "nice and cool" are the original two beers they ordered rather than a new order. Students must thus decide whether the server arrives, silently, to fill an order for a second round of beers or if the couple simply goes back to drinking the first round. In either case, the imaginary clock continues tick-tick-ticking as the couple sits in what is, the students are becoming painfully aware, an uncomfortable and uncommunicative silence.

One of the likeliest locations for long periods of silence occurs where the girl asks the man, "Can't we maybe stop talking?" (214). Her insistence—that he "please please please please please please stop talking"—makes more sense if we imagine her attempts to sit and think are interrupted, periodically, by the man's continual insistence on bringing up the exhausted subject, just as it seems the conversation has, mercifully, ended (214). The conversation finally does end when the girl threatens to replace talking with screaming. At that moment, too, the server approaches and says something that, although presented in English in the text, we are to understand is spoken in Spanish and translated for the girl by the man. Communication has broken down, and from now until the last line of the story, the only talking the girl will do is through body language: a smile for the server and a smile for the man.

In the final scene, the student playing the man should take their time—about four minutes—walking around the "station" and drinking yet another drink at the bar. Meanwhile, what does the girl do back at the table? The student playing her role will have plenty of time to decide how to deliver the last line of the story and whether or not the girl does, indeed, feel "fine" (214).

The train never arrives, so we don't know whether the man and Jig will get on it; nor do we know what will happen next if they do.[6] Try as we might to parse the maddeningly ambivalent symbolism of the beaded curtain, the round white hills, or the shadows of clouds, there is no code here to be broken. What we do know, from the wonderful awkwardness that ensues when students put back into the story the silence that silent reading otherwise removes, is that language is utterly unreliable. The story's resistance to close reading is precisely what makes it an ideal text for teaching that practice, forcing students raised in the era of standardized testing to consider questions for which there are no correct answers.

A Clean, Well-Lighted Place

James Joyce called "A Clean, Well-Lighted Place" "one of the best short stories ever written" (qtd. in Kerner 561). Hemingway himself speculated that it might be his "favorite story" (qtd. in Ryan 88).[7] However, "A Clean, Well-Lighted Place" is largely unfamiliar to most students today, a circumstance that makes it a good choice for this second collaborative close reading assignment.

In the story, published in *Scribner's Magazine* in 1933 and included that same year in the collection *Winner Take Nothing,* an old man sits in the eponymous Spanish café late at night. Two waiters observe him. One, young, is impatient with the old man. The waiter does not understand the man's need to linger at the café because the waiter has a wife waiting for him at home. Another waiter, older, has more sympathy for the old man. The waiters discuss the old man's recent suicide attempt, and the ensuing dialogue presents the crux that has troubled Hemingway scholars for more than half a century.

In 1964, three years after Hemingway's death, English professor John V. Hagopian published an article in *Studies in Short Fiction* arguing that a line of dialogue in the story contained "an obvious typographical error" (144). The problem Hagopian noticed was that, if Hemingway were following the conventions of metronomic dialogue, the same waiter who provides the information that the old man's niece cut him down says to the other waiter a few lines later, "You said she cut him down" (149).[8]

Hagopian was not the first scholar to notice the problematic line, but his inquiries were the most influential. Carlos Baker, Hagopian's former teacher and Hemingway's authorized biographer, endorsed Hagopian's suggestions for emending the story, and an editor at Scribners made the change (Baker letter to Brague). Beginning with the June 1965 printing of *The Short Stories of Ernest Hemingway* and continuing in subsequent editions, the questionable line is attributed to the other waiter: "'His niece looks after him.' / 'I know. You said she cut him down'" now reads "'His niece looks after him. You said she cut him down.' / 'I know'" (1967, 381).

Archival evidence supports the correctness of the original published order of the lines, despite the crux that it creates. Both the holograph pencil manuscript and the typescript contain the lines in the order in which *Scribner's Magazine* published them. How, then, do we solve the crux? As one of my frustrated students joked, "Can we get a time machine and get ol' Hemingway up here to tell us what's going on?" A time machine would be of no help: a note from Hemingway to professor Judson Jerome in 1956 affirms the original order of the lines and says that the story makes sense to him (Thomson 34). Unfortunately for us, Hemingway did not elaborate. As Hemingway reportedly told A. E. Hotchner, "I guess the story that tops them all for leave-out was 'A Clean, Well-Lighted Place.' I left everything out of that one" (164).

Steven K. Hoffman calls the "existential" story, which offers up a paternoster to "our nada who art in nada" (150), the "thematic as well as the stylistic climax of Hemingway's career in short fiction," and he argues that "the story is not about *nada* per se but the various available human responses to it" (176, 173). Likewise, the scholarly conversation surrounding the emendation of the story concerns not only the contested line of text itself but the various responses to the emendation. As Ken Ryan notes, "The debate since the 1965 emendation has revolved around which of the two waiters knows about the old man's attempted suicide. The assumption has been that a 'truthful' answer to this question would determine the validity of the emendation. Ironically, the result of this scholarly debate has been to suggest that the question of which waiter knows about the suicide attempt may be *irrelevant* to the emendation's validity" (89).

As with the lesson plan for "Hills Like White Elephants" discussed above, my approach to teaching "A Clean, Well-Lighted Place" seeks not to lead students to the discovery of a prescribed correct answer but rather to get them to question the text, think critically, and devise their own arguments based on textual evidence.

In teaching this story in an advanced course on Hemingway or in a course for English majors on the American short story, I do not introduce it as an unstable text.[9] When students receive the day's reading—a facsimile of the story as it appeared in *Scribner's Magazine,* available free online at Unz.com—they have no reason to believe that there might be anything amiss. Students will uncover and work to resolve the seeming inconsistency for themselves.

For fun, I have sometimes taken students to our on-campus pub to complete this lesson. A campus bar is perhaps neither as clean nor as well lighted as one would like, and this field trip requires sensitivity to the appropriateness of holding class in a bar in your own campus culture, but any space with enough room for students to collaborate in small groups will do. At this point in the semester, students are already familiar with Hemingway's iceberg theory and have completed the "Hills Like White Elephants" lesson above. My lesson for "A Clean, Well-Lighted Place" raises the stakes a bit, as it asks students not only to perform the text but to participate in adapting it for that performance, and it should be presented as a graded assignment worth about as much as a typical response paper or high-value quiz.

I distribute photocopies of the story—adhering to guidelines for fair use of copyrighted materials for educational purposes—along with instructions for students to divide into groups of three or four and transcribe the story as a script for a short film or stage play. Students are asked to give the characters names and assign to them the appropriate lines. They should also include stage directions for any pauses or action between the lines. Students are to remain faithful to Hemingway's text and should refrain from rewriting any of the dialogue. The instructor may find it useful to direct students to one of the plays in their literature anthology so that they can follow the conventions of drama. The handout also instructs students to assign parts to group members and to be ready to perform a read-through of their script in the next class period. They will be instructed to use the entire class period and to finish the assignment for homework as needed. (Here collaborative documents, such as Google Drive, can prove useful.)

Students should then set to work on their scripts. If this lesson plan works as designed, they will fail utterly at the task. If a group does manage to produce a script in the allotted time, the instructor may choose to point out the inconsistencies, or may allow the group to move into "rehearsals" where they still might discover the problems themselves. The next class period, ostensibly set aside for the performances, will mostly be used for the ensuing discussion.

I have focused here on the infamous passage, but students may also notice that there are other ambiguous moments in the text. Reading "A Clean, Well-Lighted

Place" aloud in class as we did "Hills Like White Elephants" would not work because, on first pass, we have no way of knowing who speaks first: "'Last week he tried to commit suicide,' *one waiter* said" (149; emphasis added). Hemingway does not tell us if the younger or the older waiter begins this dialogue. Another ambiguous exchange soon follows: "'The guard will pick him up,' *one waiter said*" (149; emphasis added). We must look forward into the story for clues to know which waiter speaks first in these early exchanges, but in deciding who in a passage says what, students run the risk of creating more problems than they solve. For example, with Hagopian's emendation as a cautionary tale, we can see that reassigning the attribution of certain lines in one passage risks exchanging the identities of the waiters in other passages (cf. Kerner).

As with "Hills Like White Elephants," there are a number of ways to interpret the contested lines, and students should be given a chance in class discussion to explore these possibilities. For example, as far back as 1959 Otto Reinert suggested that the crux "arises from Hemingway's violation of one of the unwritten rules of the art of presenting dialogue visually" (417–18). Reinert assigns the first two lines of the passage to the young waiter ("'He's drunk now,' he said. / 'He's drunk every night'" [149]) and the last two lines to the older waiter ("'He must be eighty years old.' / Anyway I should say he was eighty'" [149]). In the intervening decades, scholars have offered other solutions to the crux as well.[10] Perhaps Hemingway even meant for the lines to be paradoxical, as Joseph Gabriel has suggested, and that by blurring the identities of the waiters he reinforces the story's theme of nothingness (cf. Hoffman 476n3).

As for me, after studying and collating the manuscript in the Ernest Hemingway Collection at the John F. Kennedy Library, the typescript at the University of Delaware, and the text in *Scribner's Magazine* (which served as setting copy for *Winner Take Nothing*), I have concluded that Hemingway's intentions will remain a mystery, though I believe Reinert's argument most closely matches the manuscript evidence. An illegible crossed-out line *appears* to offer exposition in the contested section of the manuscript. The line most in question—"I know. You said she cut him down"—*appears* to be squeezed in place more tightly than other lines of text. A few lines above, the line "He must be eighty years old" *may* end with a comma, not a period. But these are highly subjective readings of the manuscript by a scholar who desperately wants to be the one to solve the crux. Ultimately, I tell the students, I don't know. And, I tell my students, an author's intentions, in this story or in any other, are less important than they might think. What matters most when teaching this story to undergraduates is not the problems it poses to textual scholarship but rather the experience of reading and thinking critically, looking to how a single sentence, word, or even a punctuation mark can alter its meanings.

Fittingly, any "winner" here takes nothing—or, rather, *nada*. I typically award full credit to any group who, in good faith, produces a script or who, frustrated by the crux, comes to class the next day "in despair" but ready to discuss the ambiguities of the text (149).

The confusion may annoy readers who expect from Hemingway clear, journalistic prose. This view of Hemingway as a mainstream writer who follows convention rather than a modernist innovator experimenting with form has perhaps prevented scholars from accepting the possibility that Hemingway's characters speak out of turn, answer their own statements, or engage in Joycean stream-of-consciousness internal monologues. Today's students, however, more familiar with Hemingway as a long-dead canonical writer than as an icon of popular culture, may actually be quite willing to see his work as intentionally difficult, a circumstance that gives them an advantage over Baker and other scholars unable to separate text from author.[11]

In "What Is an Author?," Foucault, with some irony, quotes Samuel Beckett to ask "What matter who's speaking, someone said, what matter who's speaking" (113). This question, which we could ask about "A Clean, Well-Lighted Place," also prompts us to consider the work we, both instructors and students, are doing in the literature classroom. What is the purpose of studying literature? Do students take courses on the short story or the American survey or literary analysis so that they might discover the meaning of a handful of particular stories? Or do they take these courses that they might become perceptive readers, critical thinkers, and better writers overall? When instructors, too, demonstrate uncertainty in how to interpret a crux, they model the learning process. This "constructivist approach" to learning recognizes that the value of a liberal arts education "is not simply acquiring specific knowledge and expertise, but rather *building understanding*" (Cole 30–31; emphasis in original). If students finish reading "Hills Like White Elephants" and "A Clean, Well-Lighted Place" with more questions than answers, the lesson has been a success.

Notes

The author wishes to thank her students at the Pennsylvania State University and at Hampden-Sydney College, especially James F. Agnew IV and Ryan Haywood, for their thought-provoking questions, observations, and arguments. Hampden-Sydney is an all-male school, and out of necessity all roles in classes there were played by men. In the spirit of practicing inclusiveness and tolerance, I encourage instructors *not* to take a student's gender identity or gender presentation into consideration when assigning parts. The performances work just as well with any ratio of men, women, and nonbinary readers.

1. Theories on learning styles build upon the groundwork of David Kolb and of Howard Gardner. Any taxonomy of "learning styles" and "intelligences" will be open to criticism, and there are practical and ethical problems with trying to classify students under individual headings. I offer these studies as resources for instructors wishing to enter into the massive scholarly conversation underpinning the necessity of reaching the students who enter our college literature classrooms unprepared to do college-level work.

2. For another example of this method in practice, see Fruscione.

3. The Alcoholic Beverage Labeling Act was enacted in 1988, over a decade before most of today's college students were born. Though the amount of alcohol consumed in the story is worth noting, students should consider that alcohol was not recognized by the mainstream medical establishment as a teratogen until the early 1970s. Point students to Jones and Smith's landmark study in *The Lancet* if they are incredulous.

4. For Hemingway's assessment, see his 8 April [1933] letter to Maxwell Perkins (Spanier and Mandel). For scholarly readings about the breakdown of communication in the story, see Gillette; Portch; and Smiley.

5. I would like to acknowledge my mentor, Sandra Spanier, in whose graduate seminar I first saw the benefit of reading the story out loud. Although the lesson plan I present here—which I have expanded to include acting out the scenes in real time—has been modified for undergraduates or high schoolers, it can work, too, at the graduate level.

6. Making an argument new to the scholarly conversation, one of my students performing this exercise argued that the man does not have time in this last scene to drink the drink at the bar *and* catch the train, that when he returns to the woman she smiles at him because they have not boarded the train, which has now come and gone.

7. Ryan cites Hotchner. Hotchner, too, notes the difficulty of dramatizing Hemingway's stories: "the very thing that gives sinew" to the story "challenges the dramatization of it" (164). Hotchner, who adapted a number of Hemingway stories for television, left this story alone.

8. Unless otherwise noted, all references to "A Clean, Well-Lighted Place" are to *Scribner's Magazine* (March 1933). For an overview of the decades-long discussion of the emendation, see Ryan.

9. This assignment can be adapted to any short story, not just one with a contested text. Indeed, in an introductory course, such an approach might be advisable; students will still be required to think critically about the story in ways that will challenge them.

10. For some additional possible interpretations of who says what in the story, see Thomson.

11. Baker's letter to Brague suggests that Hemingway was not a careful proofreader and it is on these grounds that Baker endorsed Hagopian's emendation. While I disagree that Hemingway did not carefully proof his work for publication, it is true that he appears to have sent this particular set of proofs back to *Scribner's Magazine* editor Alfred Dashiell in something of a hurry (cf. Spanier and Mandel). For an account of today's students' critical distance from Hemingway, see Justice in *Teaching Hemingway and Gender.*

Works Cited

Abdoo, Sherlyn. "Hemingway's 'Hills Like White Elephants.'" *Explicator,* vol. 49, no. 4, 1991, pp. 238–40.

"Average Mathematics Score Lower and Reading Score Unchanged." The Nation's Report Card: Mathematics and Reading at Grade 12. National Assessment of Educational Progress, http://www.nationsreportcard.gov/reading_math_g12_2015.

Baker, Carlos. Letter to L. H. Brague, 9 April 1964. Carlos Baker Collection of Ernest Hemingway, box 1, folder 19, Manuscripts Division, Department of Rare Books and Special Collections, Princeton University Library.

Cole, Robert W. *Educating Everybody's Children: Diverse Teaching Strategies for Diverse Learners.* Association for Supervision and Curriculum Development, 2008.

"College Enrollment and Work Activity of Recent High School and College Graduates Summary." US Bureau of Labor Statistics Economic News Release, 26 April 2018, https://www.bls.gov/news.release/hsgec.nro.htm.

Flynn, Elizabeth A. "Gender and Reading." *College English,* vol. 45, no. 3, 1983, pp. 236–53.

Foucault, Michel. "What Is an Author." Translated by Donald F. Bouchard and Sherry Simon. *Language, Counter-Memory, Practice,* edited by Donald F. Bouchard. Blackwell, 1977.

Fruscione, Joseph. "*In Our Time* and American Modernisms: Interpreting and Writing the Complexities of Gender and Culture." *Teaching Hemingway and Gender,* edited by Verna Kale, Kent State UP, 2016, pp. 27–37.

Gardner, Howard. *Frames of Mind: The Theory of Multiple Intelligences.* Basic Books, 1983.

Gillette, Meg. "Making Modern Parents in Ernest Hemingway's 'Hills Like White Elephants' and Viña Delmar's 'Bad Girl.'" *Modern Fiction Studies,* vol. 53, no. 1, 2007, pp. 50–69.

Gilmour, David R. "Hemingway's 'Hills Like White Elephants.'" *Explicator,* vol. 41, no. 4, 1983, pp. 47–49.

Hagopian, John V. "Tidying Up Hemingway's 'A Clean, Well-Lighted Place.'" *Studies in Short Fiction,* vol. 1, 1964, pp. 140–46.

Hannum, Howard L. "'Jig Jig to Dirty Ears': White Elephants to Let." *Hemingway Review,* vol. 11, no. 1, 1991, pp. 46–54.

Hashmi, Nilofer "'Hills Like White Elephants': The Jilting of Jig." *Hemingway Review,* vol. 23, no. 1, 2003, pp. 72–83.

Hemingway, Ernest. "A Clean, Well-Lighted Place" (manuscript), Ernest Hemingway Collection, John F. Kennedy Library, box 39, folder 337.

———. "A Clean, Well-Lighted Place." *Scribner's Magazine,* March 1933. *The Unz Review: An Alternative Media Selection.* https://www.unz.com/print/Scribners -1933mar-00149/.

———. "A Clean, Well-Lighted Place" (setting copy), Ernest Hemingway Collection, John F. Kennedy Library, box 33, folder 222.

———. *Death in the Afternoon.* Scribner, 1932.

———. "Hills Like White Elephants." *The Complete Short Stories of Ernest Hemingway: The Finca Vigía Edition.* Scribner, 1987.

———. *The Short Stories of Ernest Hemingway.* Scribner, 1967.

Hoffman, Steven K. "*Nada* and the Clean, Well-Lighted Place: The Unity of Hemingway's Short Fiction." *New Critical Approaches to the Short Stories of Ernest Hemingway,* edited by Jackson J. Benson, Duke UP, 1990, pp. 91–110.

Hotchner, A. E. *Papa Hemingway.* Random House, 1966.

Jones, K. L., and D. W. Smith. "Recognition of the Fetal Alcohol Syndrome in Early Infancy." *Lancet,* vol. 2, 1973, pp. 999–1001.

Justice, Hilary Kovar. "Katie and the Pink Highlighter: Teaching Post-'Hemingway' Hemingway." *Teaching Hemingway and Gender,* edited by Verna Kale, Kent State UP, 2016, pp. 153–64.

———. "'Well, Well, Well': Cross-Gendered Autobiography and the Manuscript of 'Hills Like White Elephants.'" *Hemingway Review,* vol. 18, no. 1, 1998, pp. 17–32.

Kerner, David. "The Ambiguity of 'A Clean, Well-Lighted Place.'" *Studies in Short Fiction,* vol. 29, no. 4, 1992, pp. 561–74.

Kolb, David. *Experiential Learning: Experience as the Source of Learning and Development.* Prentice-Hall, 1984.

Portch, Stephen R. "The Hemingway Touch." *Hemingway Review,* vol. 2, no.1, 1982, p. 45.

Reinert, Otto. "Hemingway's Waiters Once More." *College English,* vol. 20, no. 8, 1959, pp. 417–18.

Renner, Stanley. "Moving to the Girl's Side of 'Hills Like White Elephants.'" *Hemingway Review,* vol. 15, no. 1, 1995, pp. 27–41.

Ryan, Ken. "The Contentious Emendation of Hemingway's 'A Clean, Well-Lighted Place.'" *Hemingway Review,* vol. 18, no. 1, 1998, pp. 78–91.

Smiley, Pamela. "Gender-Linked Miscommunication in 'Hills Like White Elephants.'" *Hemingway Review,* vol. 8, no. 1, 1988, pp. 2–12.

Spanier, Sandra, and Miriam B. Mandel, eds. *The Letters of Ernest Hemingway Volume 5 (1932-1934).* Cambridge UP, projected publication 2020.

Thomson, George H. "'A Clean, Well-Lighted Place': Interpreting the Original Text." *Hemingway Review,* vol. 2, no. 2, 1983, 32–43.

Corrupt Reading in/of Hemingway's "A Simple Enquiry"

Debra A. Moddelmog

Despite a recent upsurge of critical attention to non-normative sexuality in Hemingway's works, his short story "A Simple Enquiry," first published in *Men without Women* (1927), continues to be relatively neglected. Given this scholarly track record and the fact that the story is rarely anthologized,[1] one suspects that "A Simple Enquiry" is also rarely taught in high school or college classrooms. Yet the story has a great deal to offer the teacher interested in engaging students in a critical exploration of the practice as well as the limits of interpretation, particularly as that practice is informed by a style of reading and reasoning that arose with nineteenth-century medicine and psychiatry and is still active today. It is an interpretative practice that props up homophobic bullying in our schools, the military, and elsewhere and provides the logic for less aggressive actions such as the presumption of homosexuality applied to those who are perceived to violate gender or sexual norms. Thus, "A Simple Enquiry" might be used to introduce students not only to the elliptical style that is a trademark of Hemingway's modernist writing but also to some of the pitfalls, perils, and high stakes of interpretation as applied both to literature and life.

The story takes place in Italy during World War I inside a military hut. An Italian major, who carefully strokes some oil upon his sunburned face, leaves his desk to take a nap in an adjacent room, telling his adjutant to finish up the paperwork. When the major's orderly, Pinin, enters the outer room with some firewood for the stove, the major orders that he be sent to the back room. Lying in his bunk, the major interrogates Pinin, asking whether he's been in love with a girl, why he doesn't write the girl he claims to love, and whether he's "corrupt." Pinin says he doesn't understand what the major means, and when the major makes several attempts to clarify, "And you don't really want—," "That your great desire isn't really—," Pinin looks at the floor without answering. The major is relieved at this outcome since "life in the army was too complicated." He tells Pinin that he's "a good boy," but to be careful that someone else doesn't come along and "take" him (251). He also suggests that Pinin need not be afraid, that he won't touch him, and that he can return to his platoon but had better stay on as the major's servant where he has "less chance of being killed" (252). After Pinin leaves the major's room, the adjutant looks up at him as he "walked awkwardly" across the room and out the door: "Pinin was flushed and moved differently than he had moved when he brought in the wood for the fire" (252). The adjutant looks after him and smiles. When the major hears Pinin return to the cabin and walk across the floor with more wood in his arms, he wonders whether Pinin lied to him.

Almost every critic who has written about this story reads it as presenting at least one man who is homosexual. The most common argument is that the Italian major who asks his orderly, Pinin, about his love life and makes the simple inquiry ("Are you corrupt?") is preparing for a same-sex seduction or, at the very least, a homosexual alliance in which he, the elder homosexual, will become the protector of Pinin, the younger, less experienced, and thus more vulnerable one. In the various perspectives offered by critics, the major is homosexual, Pinin sometimes is, and the adjutant who facilitates the meeting might be as well.

One critic who argues for not pinning down the sexual identities of the three characters or even the meaning of the "simple inquiry" is Gerry Brenner, who proposes that the story focuses on a "semantic riddle" (198) revolving around the meaning and application of the term "corrupt" and a "background network of signs that require discerning reading in order to resolve the textual conundrums of character and interpretation" (198). Brenner's semiotic approach suggests that the story's characters are both sign decoders and signs themselves, with readers given the ultimate responsibility of cracking these codes even though artists "whose work is truly significant must decline to answer our inquiries. They leave us as Hemingway leaves his major, perplexed, wondering if Pinin lied to him" (205). For Brenner, the central action of the story—two men (the major and adjutant) attempting to make meaning out of Pinin's ambiguous responses, movements, and behaviors—mimics the reader's own act of interpretation.

Brenner's practice of "discerning reading" (198) suggests that instructors might introduce this story in the classroom by helping students pay careful attention to cultural assumptions that enable the interpretive options that are available to readers. For example, he lays out a horizon of possibilities for understanding the major's identity and intentions, several of which directly contradict the common reading of him as "a despicably homosexual figure" (202). Indeed, one of the possibilities that Brenner offers is that the major is "an exemplary professional figure" (202). This does not mean that the major cannot also be homosexual, but it does rely upon a series of rereadings of the same evidence that has led other critics to conjoin queerness and contemptibility. For instance, for Brenner, the major's delicate rubbing of his sunburned face with oil becomes a sign not of his unsavory effeminacy but of his dedication to his job, whereby he spends hours in the blistering sun on reconnaissance missions (202). Further, Brenner suggests, the major's inquiries into Pinin's love life might be viewed not as the prelude to a seduction but rather as a task he is required to conduct as a military officer for whom possible evidence of a subordinate's potential homosexuality has come to light (202). In other words, Brenner takes the same evidence that other critics have used to assign homosexuality to the characters and demonstrates how it can be read otherwise.

Brenner's analysis shows how Hemingway turned "sign-reading problems into a fictional forte" (196). Hemingway's stories demand that students and other readers invest time in developing and deploying interpretive skills, but, as Brenner's examination reveals, they also often ramp up the interpretive stakes by setting out a number of possibilities from which it may be impossible to draw a definitive conclusion. Teachers who include "A Simple Enquiry" on their syllabus might also want to assign Brenner's essay since it demonstrates how interpretations are made but also thwarted. It thus helps to move students to a more sophisticated level of reading in which they navigate among a variety of equally plausible options and are faced with the question of how—or whether—to pick among them.

However, Brenner's semiotic reading fails to take full notice of historical and political factors that made homosexuality itself a sign to be read on the body and in the attitudes, movements, and dispositions of a person. Thus, instructors can also use this story to teach their students not simply about the importance of understanding historical context when developing a literary interpretation, which is an important point to make but also seems a rather obvious one in our time of critical theories and practices that are grounded in the historical (e.g., new historicism, cultural studies). What instructors might also demonstrate through studying Hemingway's story is a *specific* historical lesson: how the interpretive practice modeled by the characters in the story and used by many readers to unravel its meaning finds its origins in a clinical practice that arose around the time that Hemingway wrote his story. As Lee Edelman writes, in the second half of the nineteenth and into the early twentieth century, homosexuals were "not only conceptualized in terms of a radically potent, if negatively charged, relation to signifying practices, but also subjected to a cultural imperative that viewed them as inherently textual—as bodies that might well bear a 'hallmark' that could, and must, be read" (6). Within this context, the sexual interrogation in search of a homosexual identification or confession carries multiple meanings, the importance of which can best be appreciated if we introduce students to this historical context and then ask them to consider the consequences of this reading practice for both readers who apply it and subjects who are the targets of it. In addition, by becoming aware of how this reading practice works, students might also be guided to reflect on whether Hemingway's story is actually critical of—rather than in collusion with—a sexological and societal approach that assigns categories of normality and abnormality to human bodies and desires.[2]

Given that the two central characters of "A Simple Enquiry" have been read as homosexual, it is important to help students recognize, first, that no one in the story claims that identity. Nor do they claim any of the other pseudoscientific names—such as sexual invert, urning, third sex, intermediate sex—that were advanced by sexologists in the second half of the nineteenth century to distinguish the person with "contrary sexual sensation," as the German physician Karl Westphal put it in 1869, or the *inversione sessuale* (sexual inversion) coined by the Italian forensic expert Arrigo Tamassia in 1878 (Beccalossi 55). They don't even use the dominant clinical term of the time, "perverse," which Hemingway uses in other stories (e.g., "The Sea Change") and which, as Arnold I. Davidson notes, was for early sexologists a "*shared object* of psychiatric discourse about which there were commonly recognized and fully standardized forms of reasoning," one of which was that sexual perversion was "a functional disease of [the sexual] instinct" (72). Instead, the more colloquial "corrupt" is used. The question "are you corrupt?" is thus, as the question "are you perverse?" came to be, a loaded one not simply because it pressures the person to reveal his or her secret desire but also because it prejudges that desire and the person who possesses it as immoral, sick, and depraved. The question does not offer other possibilities, such as that the orderly might be open to engaging in a same-sex encounter as a way of relieving tension in a strenuous environment or simply for the sake of pleasure. Unlike this situational possibility, in "A Simple Enquiry," "corrupt" is presented as a state of being, a derogatory synonym for homosexual, an identity.[3]

Here is where instructors might ask students to explore what's at stake for the person who acknowledges a "corrupt" identity in the place and time of the story. Such an exploration can begin through lecture, but it also might be introduced through reading assignments and discussion. The 1889 Penal Code in Italy, also known as the Zanardelli Penal Code, had stopped making private homosexual behavior between consenting adults a punishable offence (Beccalossi 36–37). However, along with other European and American physicians, Italian physicians who were conducting sexological research were advancing a new understanding of sexual "deviance," "transferring it from the realm of sin and crime, to that of health and sickness" (Beccalossi 154). Chiara Beccalossi notes that in Italy in the late 1880s, sexual inversion was officially acknowledged as a mental disorder; in addition, as elsewhere throughout Europe and the United States, a scientific methodology was developed for identifying the invert and included an examination of the body, psychological investigation, and descriptions of the invert's lifestyle (45). A delicate hand, wide hips, a mincing step, a bachelor's lifestyle, a weak or nervous constitution, an arrested body development—all of these, among other "readable" characteristics—could be signs that the man was a sexual invert, a homosexual.

The homosexual thus emerged as an effect of a particular kind of surveillance, a specialized reading practice, if you will. This is a new kind of surveillance in which bodies ostensibly reveal evidence of "perversion by studying their structural characteristics, motions, and habits" (Terry 41) and in which the "fit" or "normal" body becomes tied to the fitness and future of the nation. Military surveillance now involves not simply gauging troop security and safety as well as preparedness for battle, but also basing some of those decisions on whether a soldier has a "perverse" constitution.[4] The homosexual himself can be a security risk, given that his pathologized body and mind make him unfit to serve, according to the prevailing thought of many sexologists and psychiatrists of the time. However, as Edelman reminds us, homosexuality in this era not only becomes available to signification but also acquires the power to "signify the instability of the signifying function *per se,* the arbitrary and tenuous nature of the relationship between any signifier and signified" (6). Despite some of the sexologists' adamant declarations otherwise, bodies and behaviors do not automatically signify their sexual meaning; if they did, there would be no reason to interrogate, observe, probe, and analyze individuals until they confess or confirm their secret perverse desire; there would be no reason to wonder whether they might lie since the truth would always be written on the body.

Instructors might illustrate how this new kind of surveillance and signification of the perverse subject works by asking students to trace the way in which Pinin is read by his superior officer and how he responds to that reading. Something in Pinin's behavior and/or demeanor has led the major to ask the overwhelming question, "Are you corrupt?" Instructors might then ask: "What exactly has led the major to this interrogation?" One clue appears to be that Pinin does not write to a girl, for as the major reveals, he has read all of Pinin's letters. Pinin observes that he has "been with girls" (251), but that fails to allay the major's suspicions. The major wants to know whether Pinin has ever been in love with a girl. He appears to be making a distinction between sexual acts and sexual desires: making love to a girl is not the same as loving a girl. The former is an act of opposite-sex intimacy, which can be engaged in for all sorts of reasons, including, the major seems to infer, to mislead the suspicious; the other is a sexual instinct that tells the truth about one's desire and thus one's "normalcy" or "perversion." When Pinin assures him that he is in love with "this girl" (251), the major checks to be sure the adjutant in the outer room can't hear them and asks again whether Pinin is sure he loves "a girl" and is not "corrupt." Pinin's responses, including his silence at key moments, seem to reassure the major that Pinin is either "normal" or not open to (his) homosexual advances, and he consequently tells him he's a "good boy," but to be careful not to let someone else "take" him (251). However, at the end of the story, the major doubts his earlier reading, a hesitation that appears to be based on how Pinin walks. While (still) lying in his bed, the major hears Pinin walk across the floor to bring more firewood to the stove and wonders whether he lied. It's not clear why he might draw this conclusion from the sound of Pinin's walking except that the way Pinin walks also seems to mean something to the adjutant who looks up at him when he comes out of the major's room and watches Pinin walk "*awkwardly* across the room and out the door." The narrator tells us that Pinin was "flushed and moved *differently* than he had moved when he brought in the wood for the fire." This causes the adjutant to look after him and smile (252; emphasis added).

The meaning of Pinin's "awkward" walk, flushed face, and "different" movement is open to interpretation: has he been aroused, does he feel threatened and vulnerable, is he confused, has something about himself or about the major become clear to him, does he have a "mincing step"? I will address the meaning of these multiple possibilities shortly, but the point to make with our students is that Pinin's habits, movements, and body are being watched, listened to, and interpreted as potential evidence of his sexuality, his "corruptness." Instructors might also inform their students that readers have made the same conjecture with the major. As mentioned above, most readers have read him as "despicably homosexual" (Brenner 202), although Brenner views him more sympathetically, but still as homosexual. Readers have made this inference, first, by aligning the major with the Prussian officer in D. H. Lawrence's "The Prussian Officer," a source for Hemingway's story, even though the sexual identity of Lawrence's officer is far from clear; indeed, adding Lawrence's story to the syllabus can be an excellent way to expand the discussion about a reading practice that searches for signs of homosexuality. Another way readers have inferred the major's sexual identity is by seeking evidence of it in his behavior and words, for example, in the way he puts oil on his face; in the question he asks Pinin about whether he has ever been in love, a question which is "hardly 'military'" (Flora, 107); and in the "unction of his manner" (Waldhorn, 228–29). In short, their examination of the characters in "A Simple Enquiry" should help students understand how the sexologists taught us to read the body and its dispositions for evidence of homosexuality.

It is under these circumstances that teachers might then ask their students to imagine the situation in which Pinin finds himself. As a subordinate, only nineteen, he, too, has to be an expert reader of the situation. When the major asks Pinin to come into his bunk room and shut the door, he has to wonder about the reason for the privacy. Will this be a sexual proposition? If so, and Pinin denies the invitation, will he be punished? If he accepts it, will he also be punished? Will this be an inquisition that might end in his dismissal from the army? Will it be an examination in which his secret desire is exposed and pathologized, indeed pathologized in the act of being exposed? Will it be an examination in which his body, his gestures, or his responses might be misinterpreted, and he will end up pathologized regardless of his "true" desire? Of course the proposition that might lead to sex has often been hard to distinguish from the proposition that might lead to violence, especially for those who are sexual minorities or suspected of being so, but the added threat for Pinin is that he is being interrogated under the category "corrupt" for which, at the time of the story, there is a whole set of disciplinary consequences, including psychological ones. Pinin's position thus demands dissembling because *whatever* the major's motive may be, he cannot abide the consequences.

In this reading, the indirection, the ambiguity, and the endless deferral of an answer to the question "are you corrupt?" suggest that "A Simple Enquiry" is about the resistance to sexological surveillance and authority, especially as that authority resides in the ability to coerce a confession and assign perverse meaning to the smallest gesture, omission (not writing a girl), or bodily attribute. Pinin is not the only one who evades answering this question. The major evades it as well, even though many readers have imagined they know the answer. We cannot be sure of anyone's sexual identity in the story because the signs that are supposed to reveal it are ultimately indecipherable. To bring this point home, teachers might ask students to consider how hands function in the story.

When Pinin stands before him, the major looks "down and up him, and at his hands," and asks questions that he cannot finish, "And you don't really want—," "That your great desire isn't really—" (251). The secrets that Pinin's hands might hold are never revealed. They are still and silent, refusing to give their owner away. Similarly, during this questioning, the major's "hands lay on the blanket" (251), a positioning that presents their ambiguous potential. Significantly, in the manuscript of the story, Hemingway has struck a line following this one that said, "They were good but unpleasant hands," an excision that favors ambiguity over precision.[5] Will the major's hands reach out to touch the orderly with desire, or will they become an instrument of violence, a disciplinary slap across the face, or a fist of disgust? At the end of the interrogation, when the major has been relieved from having to take action, his "hands were folded on the blankets," a sign that the moment for action has passed. This is confirmed as the major tells Pinin, "Don't be afraid . . . I won't touch you" (252). The hands of (potential) passion have been put away, but *which* way they were planning to move—toward pleasure or violence—if they were planning to move at all, is still unsettled.

The only thing that hands tell us in "A Simple Enquiry" is that they *might* tell us something. That they ultimately refuse to tell us anything for certain allows us to read Hemingway's story as we might read Pinin: as strategically refusing a sexological discourse and method of surveillance that produces the "corrupt" subject. Arnold I. Davidson notes that the style of reasoning that was developed by nineteenth-century sexologists is still with us (35–36), even though since 1973 the American Psychiatric Association no longer links homosexuality to disease, mental illness, or lack of "fitness." This style attributes sexual identity to "impulses, tastes, aptitudes, satisfactions, and psychic traits" (35). It also attributes it to gestures, movements, linguistic mannerisms, appearances, postures, physical characteristics, and ways of being in the world.

Pinin might stand for any subject whose desire has been optioned into a yes or no answer to the "simple enquiry" "are you corrupt?"—even in cases where corruptness (or perversion) and homosexuality are no longer aligned.[6] He might also stand for the child on the playground whose classmates taunt him with homophobic slurs for walking a particular way or not being athletic enough, a taunting that depends not only on reading the male body for signs of "inadequate masculinity" but also on presuming there's something wrong with that or with being gay. The approach to teaching "A Simple Enquiry" offered here gives students an in-depth look at Hemingway's elliptical, iceberg style and the modernist invitation it makes for readers to engage in the production of meaning. But it also encourages students to recognize how the interpretive invitation of this particular story is connected to the normalizing practices that not only identified but created the "corrupt" homosexual. This "lesson" could help students learn to reread (unread) and reconsider the ethical effects of a reading practice that has been with us for a very long time. It may also be a way to involve them in a conversation about whether the popular view of Hemingway as ultra-masculine and unsympathetic to queer sexualities might actually be misleading. To put this another way, students might ultimately consider whether Hemingway's story itself is a call to "corrupt" the practice of reading for corruption.

Appendix

Assignments and Resources for Teaching "A Simple Enquiry"

1. Have students read the selections included under "Homosexualities" in Bland and Doan's *Sexology Uncensored*. Discuss with them how the arguments of these sexologists continue with us today but also what has changed. Pay particular attention to Havelock Ellis's work, which Hemingway read, although it's not clear that he read *Sexual Inversion*, the work that is excerpted in Bland and Doan. Instructors might also explore the differences and debates among the sexologists, which demonstrate that homosexuality was not a self-evident category but was constructed.

2. Ask students to read D. H. Lawrence's "The Prussian Officer" and Sherwood Anderson's "Hands," both of which are sources for Hemingway's story. Mapping out similarities and differences among the three stories can be illuminating, but instructors might also focus on the way in which presumptions of homosexuality (about Lawrence's captain and Anderson's Wing Biddlebaum/Adolph Myers) can lead to particular conclusions about the central characters. Or examine how specific behaviors or characteristics (e.g., how hands function) might lead to presumptions of homosexuality. What are the problems with making such links? How else might we read these behaviors or characteristics? To what extent would it be accurate to say that Lawrence, Anderson, and Hemingway are all concerned with the blurred line between the homosocial and the homosexual, and the anxiety that this blurring creates for those who are uncomfortable with homosexuality? Each story also presents professional situations in which an older man is in charge of a younger man or boys (as is the case in Anderson). What effect does this age difference have on the issues the stories raise?

3. To engage students in the "sign decoding" process of interpretation described in this essay and outlined in some detail by Brenner in "A Semiotic Inquiry," divide them into three groups, with each group assigned a different character in the story: the major, the adjutant, and Pinin. Ask students to consider what they know about each character based on the information given by (1) the narrator, (2) the other two characters, and (3) the character himself— what he says or does. At what point are these characters making assumptions about the others? At what point do students' own assumptions enter into the sign-decoding process? What is the difference between an assumption and an interpretation? Where are students' efforts at decoding thwarted or challenged? What do students (or any readers) do when they reach an impasse or contradiction in deciphering a particular "sign"?

4. Ask students to do some research on one or more of the following topics and then explain how their findings enhance their understanding of Hemingway's story: (1) homosexuality in the United States and/or Italian military, especially during World War I; (2) sexology and homosexuality at the turn of the twentieth century; (3) the situation of bullying in today's middle and high schools, especially around (perceived) gender and sexual "otherness."

Here are some sources that can get them started on these subjects:

Homosexuality in the United States and Italian Military
Benadusi, Lorenzo. *The Enemy of the New Man: Homosexuality in Fascist Italy,* translated by Suzanne Dingee and Jennifer Pudney. U of Wisconsin P, 2012. (includes some historical information about pre–World War II Italian military)
Bérubé, Allan. *Coming Out Under Fire: The History of Gay Men and Women in World War II,* 20th anniversary edition. U of North Carolina P, 2010. (includes some discussion of the difference in treatment of gay men and women in the military before 1940)
Shilts, Randy. *Conduct Unbecoming: Gays and Lesbians in the US Military.* St. Martin's, 1993.

Sexology and Homosexuality at the Turn of the Twentieth Century in the United States and Italy
Beccalossi, Chiara. *Female Sexual Inversion: Same-Sex Desires in Italian and British Sexology, c. 1870–1920.* Palgrave Macmillan, 2012.
———. "Sexual Deviancies, Disease, and Crime in Cesare Lombroso and the 'Italian School' of Criminal Anthropology." *Disease and Crime: A History of*

Social Pathologies and the New Politics of Health, edited by Robert Peckham, Routledge, 2014.

Chauncey, George. *Gay New York.* Basic Books, 1995.

D'Emilio, John, and Estelle B. Freedman. *Intimate Matters: A History of Sexuality in America,* 3rd edition. U of Chicago P, 2012.

Duggan, Lisa. *Sapphic Slashers: Sex, Violence, and American Modernity.* Duke UP, 2000.

Hatheway, Jay. *The Gilded Age Construction of American Homophobia.* Palgrave Macmillan, 2003.

Somerville, Siobhan. *Queering the Color Line: Race and the Invention of Homosexuality in American Culture.* Duke UP, 2000.

Terry, Jennifer. *An American Obsession: Science, Medicine, and Homosexuality in Modern Society.* U of Chicago P, 1999.

Bullying

Blackburn, Mollie. *Interrupting Hate: Homophobia in Schools and What Literacy Can Do about It.* Teachers College, 2012.

Cassada, Raychelle, et al. *The Bullying Workbook for Teens.* Instant Help, 2013.

Hirsch, Lee, et al. *Bully: An Action Plan for Teachers, Parents, and Communities to Combat the Bullying Crisis.* Weinstein, 2012. (See also http://www.thebullyproject.com/.)

Vaccaro, Annemarie, et al. *Safe Spaces: Making Schools and Communities Welcoming to LGBT Youth.* Praeger, 2012.

Notes

1. The story has appeared in *In Another Part of the Forest: An Anthology of Gay Fiction,* edited by Alberto Manguel and Craig Stephenson (Three Rivers Press, 1994).

2. There are numerous accounts of the shift in the nineteenth century whereby "Sex became a complicated whole of bodily characteristics, attitudes, and character features, and sexuality a complex of behaviors, experiences, feelings, desires, and fantasies" (Oosterhuis 40–41), the most famous of which is Michel Foucault's *The History of Sexuality.* See also Oosterhuis; Davidson; and Terry.

3. Schaffner points out that "the perversions that Krafft-Ebing, Freud, Alfred Binet, Havelock Ellis, Magnus Hirschfeld, Iwan Bloch, and their sexological colleagues firmly planted into the modernist matrix include homosexuality, sadism, masochism, fetishism, voyeurism and exhibitionism," but after the Oscar Wilde trials in 1895 and the Eulenburg affair in Germany (1907–9), homosexuality took center stage, becoming the "most discussed of the perversions": "The homosexual was turned into the new

emblem of moral corruption, a figure to be feared and contained, but also one that was celebrated as a challenger of the existing sexual order" (10, 13).

4. Although the story takes place in Italy, it might be helpful to note that in the United States, the punishment of homosexual soldiers was "first codified in American military law" during World War I. This codification was facilitated by the arguments of psychiatrists, who advanced the view that homosexuality was a disease (Shilts 15–16).

5. Hemingway also made the description of Pinin more ambiguous. In the manuscript, he originally referred to Pinin as "a good-looking boy with a weak face" (Hemingway Collection, item 694, 2); however, he changed this to "a dark-faced boy," thereby eliminating two descriptors that might have provided stronger suggestions of Pinin's homosexuality. "A weak face" is an obvious link to the kind of sexological thinking that delineated the sexual invert; "good looking" would explain why the major later suggests that Pinin be careful that he not allow someone else to "take" him. But the point is that, once again, Hemingway revised in favor of ambiguity.

6. Some of the early sexologists, for example, Havelock Ellis, whose work Hemingway first read in the 1920s, attempted to present a more positive argument about homosexuality, suggesting that it was "a congenital abnormality," like color hearing, which, because of its innateness and unchangeability, should not be criminalized; it was "an aberration from the usual course of nature" (Ellis and Symonds 206, 222). Eventually Ellis disavowed the term "perversion" as applied to sexual deviations. By 1933 he declared that despite his best efforts to use the word only under protest and with an effort to neutralize its negative associations, it always carried a moral judgment. Thus the word "perversion," Ellis acknowledged, has "unfortunate results on those persons who are told they have been guilty of 'perversion'"; it is "completely antiquated and mischievous, and should be avoided" (Ellis 148).

Works Cited

Beccalossi, Chiara. *Female Sexual Inversion: Same-Sex Desires in Italian and British Sexology, c. 1870–1920*. Palgrave Macmillan, 2012.

Bland, Lucy, and Laura Doan. *Sexology Uncensored: The Documents of Sexual Science.* U of Chicago P, 1999.

Brenner, Gerry. "A Semiotic Inquiry into Hemingway's 'A Simple Enquiry.'" *Hemingway's Neglected Short Fiction: New Perspectives*, edited by Susan F. Beegel, UMI Research Press, 1989, pp. 195–207.

Davidson, Arnold I. *The Emergence of Sexuality: Historical Epistemology and the Formation of Concepts*. Harvard UP, 2001.

Edelman, Lee. *Homographesis: Essays in Gay Literary and Cultural Theory*. Routledge, 1994.

Ellis, Havelock. *Psychology of Sex: A Manual for Students*. Emerson, 1937.

Ellis, Havelock, and John Addington Symonds. *Sexual Inversion: A Critical Edition*, edited by Ivan Crozier, Palgrave Macmillan, 2008.

Flora, Joseph M. *Reading Hemingway's* Men without Women: *Glossary and Commentary.* Kent State UP, 2008.

Hemingway, Ernest. "A Simple Enquiry." *The Complete Short Stories of Ernest Hemingway: The Finca Vigía Edition,* Scribner, 1987.

———. "A Simple Enquiry" (typescript), Ernest Hemingway Collection, John F. Kennedy Library, box MS58, item 694.

Lawrence, D. H. "The Prussian Officer." *The Prussian Officer and Other Stories.* Duckworth, 1914.

Oosterhuis, Harry. *Stepchildren of Nature: Krafft-Ebing, Psychiatry, and the Making of Sexual Identity.* U of Chicago P, 2000.

Schaffner, Katharina. *Modernism and Perversion.* Palgrave Macmillan, 2012.

Shilts, Randy. *Conduct Unbecoming: Gays and Lesbians in the U.S. Military.* St. Martin's, 1993.

Terry, Jennifer. *An American Obsession: Science, Medicine, and Homosexuality in Modern America.* U of Chicago P, 1999.

Waldhorn, Arthur. *A Reader's Guide to Ernest Hemingway.* Farrar, 1972.

Filling in the Blanks

Teaching Critical Reading and Writing Using

"Paris 1922" and "The Snows of Kilimanjaro"

Hilary Kovar Justice

Too often at the end of a semester, I stare at a set of final essays—supposedly representing my students' "best" work, the culmination of months of vibrant and vigorous class discussion of which we're all justifiably proud—and I feel like I've failed.

I know my students are passionate, engaged readers. I know they've made great strides in thinking and learning about literature and culture. I know the level they're capable of, and its absence casts a pall. Not because their work is terrible (it's really not), but because the subtleties, nuances, and profound insights into texts, cultures, and contexts we've achieved collectively in class discussion are, so often, missing from their projects. Poof. Gone. Where are the students whose personalities and idiosyncrasies I've come to know and admire over the previous months? Why are they erased within these pages, pages for which the kindest description is "boring"?

After reading five or so, my descriptions become markedly less benevolent. After twenty, I'm wondering why I didn't go to law school.

This isn't to denigrate or lambast my students or, curmudgeon-like, swear things were better in "my" day when we took our lit crit straight, no chaser, uphill both ways. They've all got hearts, minds, curiosity, passion, and potential. No, the problem is (hopefully *was*) me. Partly me in my role of symbolic representation of professional acculturation (anxiety of influence), but mostly me in my role of teacher, having said, once again, "Okay, great. We've all just spent forever talking about wallpaper, furniture, and window curtains. For your final exam, here's a log, a saw blade, and a couple of nails. Build a house."

"But—"

"No buts."

No wonder the results tend not to resemble houses.

When presented with a large enough data set of failure (again, mine), I have a perverse reaction: I make things much, much harder to get at the core of the thing.[1] In an introductory class, requiring a portfolio on "The Snows of Kilimanjaro" is a bit like teaching basic swimming technique by gesturing toward the English Channel and saying, "France is that way. Go."

This may sound even more like the pedagogy of cruelty than that in the "build a house" analogy, but three things reverse that ruling: When faced with the English Channel, there's no shame in admitting that you don't know how to swim. More importantly, there's a reality in the humanities: the water's not that deep. "This isn't neurosurgery," I tell my students. "What's the worst that can happen?"

"We can fail!"

Which brings me to the third thing: "how about we agree that you're not going to fail?"

"You can do that?"

"I am Oz, the great and powerful."

"Very funny, Dr. J."

"Seriously. If you start to freak out, stand up (not that deep), take a breath, wave your hand, and we'll get whatever it is sorted."

"We still might fail."

"I've never in my life failed a student who's done the work, and I'm not going to start now."

This pedagogy of the impossible reflects my personal take on education generally and the humanities in particular; even so, my greatest ally in the introductory classroom is Ernest Hemingway.[2] Easy to read, but not easy to figure out; harder still to talk about, even harder to write about, much less coherently. Slippery devil. Really had a way with words though. "For sale: Baby shoes. Never worn." Hard to beat that.

Although some think I teach Hemingway because I'm too politically atavistic to know any better, how I actually use Hemingway in my literature and culture classrooms is best evident in this dialogue, distilled from nearly twenty years of teaching Hemingway's short fiction:

"I read it, but I don't get it."

"I know. Nothing happens!"

"Why do we have to read this [expletive]? This isn't relatable."

Eventually, some courageous soul admits, "It makes me feel stupid," to which I reply, "You're not. Not at all. You're just reading too quickly."

Exercise 1: One True Sentence

At this point, I tell the story of Hemingway's "lost manuscripts," which he writes about in *A Moveable Feast,* and the exercise he purportedly set himself: to write "one true sentence [. . .] the truest sentence that you know" (12). There is something about the lost manuscripts story that students find "relatable" (a word I find troubling but whose reality I work within): they have all had computers die, or forgotten to save, or had printers fail at critical moments.

I then tell students that Hemingway wrote six of these "true" sentences and titled them "Paris 1922" (they were first published by biographer Carlos Baker [91]). I put one of them on the board, writing only one word or phrase at a time (breaks indicated by vertical bars) and asking with each new word or phrase what the effect is (how they feel, how it works) and what comes next (an actual prediction or sometimes which part of speech).

I | have seen | the one-legged streetwalker | who | works | the Boulevard Madeleine | from the Rue Cambon to Bernheim Jeune's | limping | through the crowd | on a | rainy | night | with | a beefy | red-faced | Episcopal clergyman | holding | an umbrella over her.[3]

"'I.' Why 'I'?" I ask.
"Well, it's a true sentence, so of course it begins with I."
"So truth is subjective?"
We talk about that for a while. Then, "Why 'streetwalker'? Why not 'whore' or 'prostitute'? What work does this word do that its synonyms don't?"
"Oh . . . 'one-legged' versus 'walking.'"
"Is that why you all laughed?"
"Um . . . yeah . . ."
"Why 'Madeleine'?"
"Because it's the actual street name?"
"Well, sure, but let's pretend we're English majors for a moment; we can do more with that."
Eventually someone (occasionally prompted by asking whether anyone speaks French or is familiar with the Bible) spots the "Magdalene" reference. "Oh. Oh!"

"Limping" transforms the objectifying laughter of "streetwalker" into the beginnings of pity.

"Beefy" raises alarm; the former object of laughter turned object of pity is now in danger, and pity becomes compassion.

They're invested now. "What comes next?"

"No, I think I'm done."

"That's mean!"

"Fine, fine . . . here's the next phrase."

"Episcopal clergyman."

"Wow!" and "Wait—huh?"

"Episcopal clergyman" releases the tension created by "beefy" and demands a reconsideration of "red-faced." The record for this reconsideration is fifteen minutes. "Fifteen minutes on a single adjective," I note dryly. "Goodness. You'd think it's relatable or something."

Predicting what comes after "holding" divides students into camps: he's holding either her hand (Good Priest, if he's helping; Bad Priest, if he's her client; "Do Episcopal clergymen take vows of celibacy?" "No." "Oh, well that's okay then . . .") or his wallet (Bad Priest, unless he's giving her charity, in which case Good Priest).

Eventually, someone guesses "umbrella."

"There. Truth, from 'I' to 'umbrella.' Read more slowly," I finish, after what I always imagine will take fifteen minutes has taken nearly an entire class period.

"Wow! But do we have to read everything *that* slowly?"

"Have to? No. You *can*, but hello, time management? Your gut and experience will teach you where and when slowing to an apparent crawl might yield something you really need."

"Such as?"

"The conventional ones are the title, an epigraph, the first sentence ("convention of notice"), the exact middle ("the turn"), the last sentence. Your gut will tell you the rest."

"What's a 'turn'?"

"We'll get there. I promise." (As will this essay.)

"So 'go with your gut' is like when it's relatable?"

"No."

Exercise 2: Go with Your Gut

After the "One True Sentence" exercise, students read "The Snows of Kilimanjaro" and, without benefit of class discussion, write initial responses to them (in the form of a list of questions and brief statements), which I save for later use.[4] I call this their "First Impressions" list.

What follows condenses over two months of class time in which critical reading practices are foregrounded and cemented through repeatedly encountering new works, listing initial impressions, and group discussions. During this phase, students read several earlier (and shorter) Hemingway stories paired with stories by contemporary American writer Kirk Curnutt and chapters from Jonathan Culler's *Literary Theory: A Very Short Introduction*. This "critical reading" phase is devoted to the development of a localized discourse community.

1. Students are required read the story at least three times before class (preferably once a day, to let reflection happen organically). At the beginning of each class, I read an excerpt aloud to help everyone switch gears from their last class.

2. Students are required to come prepared with three questions or observations. These may be quotations that they found beautiful, profound, funny, particularly well worded, etc. ("Wow!"); they may be requests for assistance with moments that they found confusing or troubling ("Huh?"). I record these on the board or projector screen, and we discuss which can be easily addressed, which are probably connected, and which are absolutely crucial. Free-form discussion ensues with frequent references to other items on the "Wow!"/"Huh?" list.

For example, the "Huh?" moments in "Indian Camp" include the cigar, the death of the father, "the *other* boat" (67; emphasis added) with which the story begins, and why young Nick is called an "interne" (68). Always on the "Wow!" list is the story's last line, "In the early morning on the lake sitting in the stern of the boat with his father rowing, he felt quite sure that he would never die" (70). When discussing "Hills Like White Elephants," the "Huh?" category includes, "What happens at the end," "Why are they drinking so much?" and "Why's she called a 'girl'?" The "Wow!" moments are fewer for this story but have included "the shadow of a cloud moved across the field of grain" and "I don't care about me" (213).

As professor/moderator/she-who-provides-footnotes-as-necessary, I encourage vigorous, respectful, and enjoyable intellectual brawls, always with an eye on the text. My philosophy in class discussion is "Interesting; responses?" From the inside, this can be quite a dance (I never know what to expect); from the outside, barely controlled chaos. While the framework of the syllabus and the process-outline of the final portfolio are clearly and firmly delineated, two months of chaos proves not only valuable for its freedom but productive for its repetitive replication of the blank page that every writer confronts with every project.

Students realize that with Hemingway, the closer you look, the more ambiguity you find. Two diametrically opposing readings can both be supported by the text, and yet—by some miracle of writing—it's still a good story. Brilliant, in fact.

Early discussions tend to go like this:

"But I want to know!" the students fume, en masse. "How old is Nick *really?*" "Does she have the abortion or not?" "Is Uncle George the father?"

"Embrace the chaos."

"Huh?"

"If you want to start a brawl at a Hemingway conference, walk up to any group of scholars—smart, serious people who do this for a living—and announce flat-out that Uncle George is the baby's father."

"So we can just make it up?"

"No."

Perhaps the most valuable lesson students learn from early-semester discussions is that sometimes to find a smart answer you have to ask the (supposedly) "stupid" question. "Wait—who's this story *about?* Nick? Uncle George? Dr. Adams? Or the woman?"

"What if it's more broadly about gender?"

"Or race?"

"Or coming of age?"

Over weeks of discussing new stories, student responses move inexorably from certainty to subtlety, from the concrete to the flexible, from believing that "What's it about?" has a single, unified answer that resides in the ether to noting how women are doubly silenced by racist culture, how maturity begins with a self-conscious decision, or how you can't protect your kid from life.

"Are we just making it up?" I ask occasionally.

"Duh, Dr. J. It's supported by the text."

Final Portfolio Project: "The Snows of Kilimanjaro"

Finally, students embark on a four-week final portfolio project on "The Snows of Kilimanjaro," a story selected because of its "make it harder" features, including relatively greater length, ambiguity, the pertinence of biographical material, structural complexity, extant archival resources, political hot points, and especially the extent to which it benefits from and repays their concerted effort and weeks of practice reading Hemingway's shorter and earlier stories.[5] This four-week period is intended to break down a set of steps that enable students to see very clearly how critical writing capitalizes on critical reading. This clarity has the added bonus of illustrating how students risk curtailing their own thoughts when they write their final essay the night before.

To initiate the project, I return students' "First Impressions" lists and ask them to reread "The Snows of Kilimanjaro" and prepare two written pieces: "Second Impressions" and a short statement briefly comparing their first and second impressions of the story. Most of them report that although their emotional responses to the story have not changed, their written responses are more specifically targeted to textual moments and broadened to include questions of writing, the writer, and wording. Questions concerning characters' motivations and "What's it about?" remain, but awareness of the "written-ness" of the text is heightened; questions and lists tend to be longer. Nearly all students maintain that although they know they're reading more closely and more analytically, they're still not sure "what to do" with the story, and could we perhaps get started on final projects, please?

"You're sure you don't want to wait 'til the night before?"

"Get real, Dr. J."

Their preparation for and of the critical essay involves working through a very formulaic set of steps (guidelines, not mandates) that offers one way to approach critical academic writing. Not the only way, certainly—just one way. The guidelines, I tell students, provide one successful architectural frame on which to drape their own individual readings of a text according to what they feel (yes, *feel*) are its most compelling aspects. Whatever they find important *is* important; the portfolio project foregrounds the "how"—a "how" that they can then modify, refine, translate, or reject entirely as they continue with their education. My philosophy here is that a solid "how" will support many a variant "what," and that affirming every student's individual (textually supported) "what" will go a long way toward keeping the human in the humanities.

Perhaps I digress.

The last four weeks of my introductory class breaks down one constitutive approach to an analytical argument into four elements:

1. WHAT (generated individually; emotional/intellectual; text-supported)
2. TURN (convention of narrative; student-located; text-supported; a gut-check opportunity)

3. HOW (generated individually; analytical; supported by logic and text)
4. SO WHAT? (synthesis of the first three items in this list; highly individual)

After a relatively brief group discussion of the story based on their second impressions lists, I ask students to write down what they, at the gut level, believe are the three most important concepts in the story. While their lists almost always include at least one of the story's "big three" (marriage, writing, death/dying), I've never seen two identical lists. "Memory" appears with some frequency, as do "regret," "spirituality," "nature," and "despair."

I then ask them to consider the first three concepts and to identify some sort of larger unity among them. This proves challenging; students concerned with "right answers" require affirmation that this is up to them. I sometimes help them refine their thinking through conversation—for example, "Do you mean 'despair' in the religious sense of 'loss of faith,' or do you mean 'despair' in the more secular sense of 'hopelessness'?"

At every point in the process, I remind students that they can always alter or abandon their earlier conclusions. "After looking for a unity, I think what I meant by 'writing' was really 'creativity.' Is that okay?" Yes. "I think what I meant by 'women' was actually 'relationships'—can I use that instead?" Of course. "I can't quite differentiate between 'God' and 'nature' in this. Can I toss out my earlier one and use both of them?" Absolutely.

All of this saying "yes" makes for a great time in the classroom.

"So how are you all doing?"

"Got the concepts, got the unity, *still* don't know what to do with the story!"

I then share with them one place I often start, perhaps the single most useful thing I ever learned in a literature class: the "turn," or the "narrative pivot."[6] When I'm working to understand a conventional Western narrative, I look for the "turn"—a moment that occurs at or really close to the mathematical middle of a narrative that isolates the larger, overarching stakes. The definition I write on screen is this: the moment at which that which was previously only possible becomes either _____ or _____.

We then discuss what works in those blanks; eventually they're filled in with "inevitable" or "impossible."

"So the mathematical middle?" they ask.

"Yep. It's wild, but it works."

"Where's your textual evidence, Dr. J.?"

I love it when the tables turn. "I learned it from a Shakespeare scholar; in Shakespeare it's sometimes called 'the 3.2 turn' because Act 3, Scene 2 is usually

where it happens—and that's usually the exact middle of the play. Let's take
Julius Caesar. The 3.2 turn is Caesar's murder."

"Okay, but that's Shakespeare. What about stuff everyone reads?"

"Doesn't everyone read Shakespeare? Okay, okay. Does *Harry Potter*
qualify?"

Nods.

"Okay. What's the mathematical middle of the series?"

"Book 4 [*Harry Potter and the Goblet of Fire*]."

"Anything big happen in that one?"

"Voldemort returns . . . which . . . oh! Which makes the final confrontation
inevitable! Wow!"

"I don't think writers consciously think, 'Now I need a turn,'" I continue. "I
suspect we all, writers and readers, internalize culturally determined patterns—
not necessarily good, not necessarily bad—and we're hegemonically trained to
instinctively expect them."

"Like when you know the chorus is coming after the bridge?"

"Exactly."

Students then reread "The Snows of Kilimanjaro" (this is the third official
time), looking specifically for a single sentence or even a paragraph break that
constitutes the turn. They write these down and cast their ballots; I read them
aloud. In my experience, 90 percent of them identify this sentence: "It came
with a rush; not as a rush of water nor of wing; but of a sudden evil-smelling
emptiness and the odd thing was that the hyena slipped lightly along the edge
of it" (47). The other 10 percent select the sentence before: "And just then it
occurred to him that he was going to die" (47). What's noteworthy is the utter
lack of outliers.

Regardless, consensus isn't required; any student-selected sentence that
fits the criteria will work in what comes next: students return to their three
concepts (see p. 106) and select for each two quotations from the story (one
pre-turn, one post-turn), which speak most eloquently to them. These selections are referred to as their "paired sentences."

They're then asked to consider how those sentences work as writing—what
are the patterns they see among all six? This requires some creativity, some
thought, and often conversation (in person or over email). The patterns—which
we call "the How"—can be almost anything—from grammar to structure to
denotative content. "Before the turn, they're dialogue; after the turn, they're
internal." Or "All of them come immediately after the italicized sections." Or
"Before the turn, all the verbs are active; afterwards, passive." "Before, they're

all about his wife; after, they're all about nature." Sometimes they don't map neatly. "All the ones about creativity and memory work one way; the ones about death work in the opposite way." Whatever "how" students locate, hone, and refine to their satisfaction is the one they'll work with in the critical essay.

Next they're asked to fill in the blanks to generate their own "true sentence": In "The Snows of Kilimanjaro," Hemingway [verb] [THREE CONCEPTS], [verb] [UNITY], by [HOW].

Granted, this part of the exercise is formulaic, but by the time they write it, each student's reading (and thus the sentence they generate) is unique. The fill-in-the-blank exercise provides a foundational touchstone for them as writers, and they spend days selecting the right words for a single sentence whose content they find accurate and satisfying.

Days, on one true sentence.

Finally, they're asked to describe, in writing, however many connections they can see between their own true sentence and the following story elements:

- title
- epigraph
- first sentence
- turn (student identified)
- last sentence
- their three paired sentences

These descriptions are both exploratory and explanatory; they constitute the foundation of their critical essay.

The organization of the essay is up to them. Therein lies one of the "make it harder" challenges: the elements they're required to address defy easy organization. How to mesh and balance the story's organization (which itself depends on flashbacks and a dying vision) with their paired pre- and post-turn sentences; how to mesh and balance Hemingway with themselves is a problem they must solve individually.

They always have one more question: "How long does it have to be?"

"As long as it takes."

"But . . ." (or sometimes, "Yay!")

"*Harry Potter* is seven books long. 'For sale: Baby shoes' is six words. Aim more for Hemingway than Rowling; you only have so much time."

By now they realize that the last four weeks are what we sometimes leave until the night before; they realize that temporarily adhering to formulaic architecture allows for proper emphasis on their "Wow!," their "Huh?," and their "So What?" In other words, on their truth.

This approach may seem uncomfortably like a return to close reading in service of a five-paragraph essay; there are elements of that formula lurking about, to be sure. But what's defined here is only the architecture—a framework whereupon they, as unique readers, can rock my world, and a start on which to build in their future classes. This is but the first course they'll take in this discipline, not the last; I trust both my students and colleagues with evolution. This approach is predicated on three assumptions: that students want to learn, that they want and deserve to be respected as human beings, and that they want to succeed.

It results in portfolios in which their strengths and weakness are obvious to both student and professor, standing out in obvious bas relief against a simple background. It results in essays that sound a bit more like "professional writing with heart" than a lot of heart and talent in search of a point or, worse, something hollow and performative that bores first them, then me.

They go forth armed with earned confidence and proven skills.

And I have fewer fantasies about law school.

Notes

1. Although I currently teach undergraduate English majors, I learned the benefits of making things harder while teaching high school sophomores.

2. Sometimes it's William Shakespeare, Gertrude Stein, or J. K. Rowling.

3. I have lifted this exercise from Paul Smith's 1994 Hemingway class at Trinity College; it works in high school, university, and graduate classrooms and equally well in writers' workshops.

4. I am indebted to William Veeder for the "go with your gut" advice.

5. I have also used William Faulkner's "The Bear," which fulfills similar criteria, in this role in earlier iterations of this course and more advanced literature courses. My decision to modify my introductory syllabus to focus more closely on Hemingway was due to two factors: the availability and pertinence of several extratextual archival sources, particularly the *Look* magazine essays Hemingway wrote of his own near-death experience in Africa, and the opportunities offered by Kirk Curnutt's contemporary short fiction in the collection *Baby, Let's Make a Baby*, several of which offer strong echoes of or pose overtly crafted responses to specific Hemingway stories.

6. I am indebted to Arthur Feinsod's 1995 Shakespeare course at Trinity College for the concept of "the turn"; the definition I use in class has evolved over time.

108   HILARY KOVAR JUSTICE

Works Cited

Baker, Carlos. *Ernest Hemingway: A Life Story.* Collier Books, 1969.

Hemingway, Ernest. "Hills Like White Elephants." *The Complete Short Stories of Ernest Hemingway: The Finca Vigía Edition.* Scribner, 1987.

———. "Indian Camp." *The Complete Short Stories of Ernest Hemingway: The Finca Vigía Edition.* Scribner, 1987.

———. *A Moveable Feast.* Touchstone, 1996.

———. "The Snows of Kilimanjaro." *The Complete Short Stories of Ernest Hemingway: The Finca Vigía Edition.* Scribner, 1987.

"The Short Happy Life of Francis Macomber," Theory, and the Systematic Literature Review

Cam Cobb

Hemingway's first two books were short story collections, and his better-known stories from these collections continue to capture the imagination of seasoned as well as emerging literary critics. The sheer volume of new and old writing on Hemingway's short fiction can be daunting for the budding scholar, and it can make our work as teachers challenging. How can we possibly expect our students to make sense of all the critiques on Hemingway's well-trodden (and even his lesser-known) stories? To achieve this task, it is useful to help students shift from the haphazard approach of carrying out non-systematic literature reviews (NSLRs) to developing and honing their skills in conducting systematic literature reviews (SLRs) (Boote and Beile; Evans and Kowanko; Randolph).

In this chapter I map out a way of guiding students through the process of learning how to carry out an SLR and understanding when and why it would be suitable to do so. Imagine that I am teaching a class of approximately twenty-five third- and fourth-year undergraduate students. Class sessions are three hours long and are held once a week. Students are, for the most part, literature majors, yet a few are taking this course as an elective and come from other faculties and departments. Through their experiences, many of the students have encountered a variety of theoretical lenses that may be used to analyze works of fiction, such as feminist theory, Marxism, ecocriticism, and critical race theory (see, for instance, Tyson).

For students in this context, the SLR has much to offer. It is a process that involves setting out a clear research design when gathering, selecting, and analyzing a body of research. When conducting an SLR, scholars articulate *where* studies will be found as well as *how* they will be selected and analyzed. Methodological decisions, such as selecting search engines and using search terms, are explained along the way. Scholars then outline (and rationalize) a set of selection criteria that would winnow down the pool of studies that has been gathered. By explaining key research decisions made throughout this process, scholars take an approach that is both transparent and rationalized. When taking an aerial view of a body of research and striving to understand the patterns within that body of research, the SLR is indispensable. It pushes scholars to move beyond choosing favorites or cherry-picking studies that support an argument or interpretation. When discussing the benefits of the SLR, Boote and Beile noted, "To advance our collective understanding, a researcher or scholar needs to understand what has been done before, the strengths and weaknesses of existing studies, and what they might mean. A researcher cannot perform significant research without first understanding the literature in the field" (3).

While outlining this teaching endeavor, I focus on Hemingway's 1936 story, "The Short Happy Life of Francis Macomber"—a narrative that has garnered an immense and rather diverse array of scholarship over the years. To this end, I have organized this article into three parts: teaching philosophy, teaching-learning context, and teaching the systematic literature review.

Teaching Philosophy

It is important to begin with my teaching philosophy. After all, it underpins everything that follows in this chapter. There are three pillars that inform my teaching practice, namely constructivism, engagement, and critical pedagogy.

According to constructivists, educators must strive to understand the perspectives, experiences, motivations, wants, hopes, and needs of learners. Yet constructivism is more than this. In addition to understanding students, educators must *respond* to them. Within this framework, teaching becomes an act of reciprocity and dialogue. For John Dewey, education is not simply a matter of replicating preplanned tasks that are repeated year after year; rather, it is an ongoing process of designing and then facilitating the right *sorts* of experiences. As he wrote in *Experience and Education* (1938), "[T]he central problem of an education based upon experience is to select the kind of present experiences that live fruitfully and creatively in subsequent experiences" (27–28). He went on to explain, "There must be a reason for thinking that [learning materials and methods] will function in generating an experience that has educative quality with particular individuals at a particular time" (46). Here, it is vital that students have a voice, make decisions, and become actively engaged in their education.

Engagement marks the second key aspect of my teaching. For students to develop skills that are meaningful, they need to be immersed in challenges where they have agency. Rather than passively responding to prescriptive drills, students need to have choices and a real stake in the construction of the tasks they are expected to complete. Moreover, the learning tasks should be ones that compel students to wrestle with ideas, challenges, contradictions, and complexities. Brazilian activist and philosopher Paulo Freire viewed dialogue and what he called "problem-posing education" as a way of countering the dulling effects of teacher-centered education. For Freire, the notion that teachers provide students with deposits of knowledge—what he called "banking education"—is contradictory to learning. Banking education encourages a vertical relationship of domination and hinders opportunities for students to teach and teachers to learn. As Freire noted, "The role of the problem-posing educator is to create; together with the students" (81).

As important as constructivism and student engagement are, they do not fully capture my philosophy of teaching. Teaching and learning—actions that interlock with one another—are distinctly political. Educators help students to form their own way of reading and making meaning of the world—and the world itself is governed by political conditions, power relations, and social in/justices. It is a key axiom of critical pedagogy.

When teachers lay claim to neutrality and avoid discussing topics that are in any way remotely political, that is itself a political act—and it conveys a message that political conditions, power relations, and social in/justices are unimportant or unrelated to what is being learned. Freire rejected this claim, reasoning that "[h]uman beings are not built in silence, but in word, in work, in action-reflection" (88). As such, when critical thinking transforms into critical pedagogy, teachers and learners consider the social conditions of different topics and phenomena—and, by extension, they consider the power systems that underpin those conditions. As Burbules and Berk noted, "When Critical Pedagogy talks about power and the way in which it structures social relations, it inevitably draws from a context, a larger narrative, within which these issues are framed" (55). As you continue reading this chapter, keep these three ideas—constructivism, engagement, and critical pedagogy—in mind. They form the basis of my approach to teaching.

Teaching-Learning Context

Students have enrolled in this course to delve into various works of twentieth-century American literature. While most are familiar with the practice of carrying out a close reading of a text, it is unlikely that any have encountered (let alone conducted) an SLR before. As such, we begin the course by collaboratively conducting a close reading of a well-known short story. Over the next few weeks, we delve into a variety of theoretical lenses—such as feminist theory, Marxism, ecocriticism, and critical race theory—to explore another landmark of twentieth-century American literature. Along the way, we critically interrogate scholarship on the text, discussing possibilities and evidence of various logical fallacies and cognitive biases in the scholarship. Throughout this process, we scaffold learning as students take on problem-based tasks and deliver short presentations using a TED Talk format (Hmelo-Silver et al.). On occasion, students expand their presentations by leading short follow-up discussions.

Because we are focusing on literary analysis and twentieth-century American fiction, I devote a sequence of lessons to teaching the SLR by way of Hemingway's short story, "The Short Happy Life of Francis Macomber" near the end of the first semester. "Macomber" is particularly suitable for teaching the SLR. It is an intriguing narrative, and—like many Hemingway stories—it is open to a variety of plausible interpretations. Moreover, the story has garnered a range of critical responses over the years. It is a text that is ripe for students to develop or hone their skills as scholars.

Teaching the Systematic Literature Review

I have taught the SLR for a few years now to graduate students in various faculties, including education, literature, and law. Rather than recounting specific experiences I have had (or approaches I have taken) in teaching the SLR, I have designed this segment of the chapter as a composite and overview of how I would use "Macomber" to teach the SLR to a class that is unfamiliar with the process. While I focus on the opening two lessons of the sequence, I close with a brief synopsis of what would unfold in the following five lessons.

Lesson 1: Exploring the Story

In this first lesson, students will begin to delve into "Macomber." Rather than telling them about the story and summarizing how it has been analyzed over the years—which would constitute a form of banking education—this experience will be exploratory in nature. Before coming to class, students will have already read the narrative as homework. Also, prior to the lesson, I instruct students to avoid any interpretations or critiques of the story—so they themselves may read, or ground, the text in their own way. As Creswell explains, constructive grounded theory "lies squarely within the interpretive approach to qualitative research with flexible guidelines, a focus on theory developed that depends on the researcher's view, learning about the experience within embedded, hidden networks, situations, and relationships, and making visible hierarchies of power, communication, and opportunity" (65). In taking this approach, students will bring an openness and transparency with them as they dig into "Macomber" while actively drawing from various theoretical lenses.

Lesson 1: Group Task

Form groups of four to five. Examine the lists of theoretical lenses and artifacts in the two lists below. With your group mates, select one item from each list. You may mix and match as you see fit, as long as you select one theoretical lens and one artifact.

Once you have made your selection, have one member of the group list the names of everyone in the group on the chalkboard. Be sure to indicate the theoretical lens and artifact your group has selected (duplication is permitted).

Using your theoretical lens and artifact, develop a TED Talk response (four to six minutes) to "Macomber." You may focus on a specific scene from the story. Your TED Talk should briefly sum up the theory, outlining how it was used to examine the story or scene. Briefly describe the artifact itself and explain how it shed light on the story in conjunction with the theory at hand. (This is an activity to get students thinking about how theories and artifacts can help them to explore various aspects of literature.) Please do not feel that you are expected to put forward a full analysis of the story. Focusing on a scene from the story would be quite suitable for this activity.

Determine who will say what beforehand so that all group members know how they will contribute. Each group member will speak for about one minute. You will have forty minutes to brainstorm and discuss before you present to the class. I will circulate, monitor, and provide constructive feedback along the way.

List 1: Theoretical Lens

- Feminism (fourth wave)
- Marxism
- Ecocriticism
- Critical Race Theory

List 2: Artifact

- YouTube video: "Elephant Hunting in Africa, 1930s," Huntley Films Archive
- Mainstream media: "Blame War, Not Safaris," *New York Times,* 29 June 2014
- Statistical research: "The Effects of Trophy Hunting on Five of Africa's Iconic Wild Animal Populations in Six Countries," Conservation Action Trust. [Because this document is rather long, students may focus their attention on a section devoted to one type of animal.]
- Blog post: "Holiday Like Hemingway in Africa," Messy Nessy. [Because web pages are prone to come and go, any of these artifacts may be replaced with similar ones.]

Following group presentations, I will lead a brief wrap-up discussion with the class exploring a variety of questions, including:

- What is a power relation you notice in the story? What plot points or bits of dialogue indicate this?
- How do certain theoretical lenses help to illuminate power dynamics you notice between different characters in the story?
- What does the story indicate about society in the 1930s?
- How would you compare the social conditions and power relations of the story to those of today?
- How have things changed since the time of the story—how have they *not* changed?

I will close this lesson by informing the class that while we have resisted looking at critical responses to "Macomber" thus far, we will begin to delve into the body of scholarship on the short story in our next lesson.

Lesson 2: Understanding the Systematic Literature Review

The second lesson will focus on the SLR—but it will begin with the NSLR. Again, rather than didactically explaining things (for example, spelling out the differences between an SLR and NSLR), I will use two resources (exemplar literature review excerpts I have written for this purpose) to get students to critique and, in doing so, actively identify drawbacks that are common to NSLRs. I will open the lesson by telling students that we are now going to look at a body of scholarship on "Macomber."

Lesson 2: Group Task 1

Yesterday you developed short responses to "Macomber" utilizing a specific theoretical lens and artifact. You then presented your responses to the class working alongside your group mates in our TED Talk format. Thus far, we have avoided delving into the scholarly responses to the text. Today we will critique excerpts of two rather different literature reviews that survey some of the scholarship on "Macomber." Let's begin with the first.

Examine the exemplar literature review excerpt below. I have designed it for you to critique. Let's say it was written by Author X. Working with your group mates, respond to two of the four question clusters below. You will then share your findings with the class. Each group will have four to six minutes to present. Determine who will say what beforehand so that all group members know how they will contribute. Again, each group member will speak for approximately one minute. I will circulate, monitor, and provide constructive feedback as you complete this task.

1. What is the research question (or set of questions) at the heart of this literature review? What is the focus of this literature review? How do you know these things?

2. How would you describe the research design of this literature review? What do you know about the author's process of developing it?

3. What would you say are the strengths and weaknesses of this literature review? How did you draw these conclusions?

4. What sorts of logical fallacies or cognitive biases can you find in this literature review?

Literature Review 1 (Excerpt)
By Author X

"The Short Happy Life of Francis Macomber" is one of Hemingway's most popular stories. It captures many of the writer's well-known tropes, including the femme fatale, the code hero, and grace under pressure. While there are certainly points of ambiguity in the text, it seems clear that Margot purposefully shoots and kills her husband at the end of the story. By that point, Francis had transformed from the cuckold coward of the narrative's opening into something quite different—something that challenged Margot. A perusal of the scholarship on "Macomber" indicates that the consensus among critics is that Margot indeed murdered her husband, as confirmed by no less than six academics, including Baker, Young, Fiedler, Stein, Waterman, and Bell. Yet responses to the story have delved into far more than Margot's culpability.

Some have examined the narrative—and particularly the actions of Robert Wilson and Francis Macomber—in relation to Hemingway's infamous code hero (Bell; Pierce). Discussing the car as a symbol in the story, Pierce noted that "Hemingway uses the car as a changing symbol to delineate his characters: the protagonist Francis Macomber, his wife Margot, and the white hunter Wilson. It serves, in part, as the motivation for Macomber's belated initiation into manhood. It illustrates Wilson's code of conduct. And it underscores Wilson's belief in the corruptive power of women as shown by Margot" (230).

Yet not all criticism focuses on Francis and Margot. More recently, scholars have dug deeper into the perspective and motives of the hapless Robert Wilson (Cheatham; Blythe and Sweet). In more recent years, scholars have considered the origins of the story (Cameron) as well as its cinematic representation (Kaplan). Perhaps it was inevitable that this well-trodden story would be discussed in the classroom context. To that end, three scholars have reflected on their use of the text as a pedagogical resource (De Fusco; Harrington; Wheeler). Undoubtedly, "Macomber" is one of Hemingway's most popular narratives, among fans and academics alike. Not only is there a wealth of criticism on the story but the scholarship itself varies greatly.

REFERENCES

Baker, Carlos. "The Two African Stories." *Hemingway: A Collection of Critical Essays,* edited by Robert P. Weeks, Prentice-Hall, 1962, pp. 118–26.

Bell, H. H. "Hemingway's 'The Short Happy Life of Francis Macomber.'" *Explicator,* vol. 32, no. 9, 1974, pp. 151–52.

Blythe, Hal, and Charlie Sweet. "Wilson: Architect of the Macomber Conspiracy." *Studies in Short Fiction,* vol. 28, no. 3, 1991, pp. 305–9.

Cameron, Kenneth M. "Patterson and the Blyths: The Originals of Hemingway's 'Macomber' Triangle." *Hemingway Review,* vol. 11, no. 2, 1992, pp. 52–55.

Cheatham, George. "The Unhappy Life of Robert Wilson." *Studies in Short Fiction,* vol. 26, no. 3, 1989, pp. 341–45.

De Fusco, Andrea. "Discussing 'Macomber' in the Undergraduate Writing Seminar: What We Talk about When We Talk about Hemingway." *Hemingway Review,* vol. 17, no. 1, 1997, pp. 72–79.

Fiedler, Leslie A. *Love and Death in the American Novel.* Criterion, 1960.

Harrington, Gary. "'Shootism' Versus 'Sport' in Hemingway's 'Macomber.'" *Teaching Hemingway and the Natural World,* edited by Kevin Maier, Kent State UP, 2017, pp. 137–48.

Kaplan, E. Ann. "Hemingway, Hollywood and Female Representation: The Macomber Affair." *Literature/Film Quarterly,* vol. 13, no. 1, 1985, pp. 22–28.

Pierce, J. F. "The Car as Symbol in Hemingway's 'The Short Happy Life of Francis Macomber.'" *South Central Bulletin,* vol. 32, no. 4, 1972, pp. 230–32.

Stein, William Bysshe. "Hemingway, 'The Short Happy Life of Francis Macomber.'" *Explicator,* vol. 19, no. 7, 1960, pp. 105–7.

Waterman, Arthur E. "Hemingway's 'The Short Happy Life of Francis Macomber.'" *Explicator,* vol. 20, no. 1, 1961, p. 5.

Wheeler, Belinda. "Redeeming Hemingway and His Women: Periodicals as Sites of Change in the Literature." *Teaching Hemingway and Gender,* edited by Verna Kale, Kent State UP, 2016, pp. 47–57.

Young, Philip. *Ernest Hemingway: A Reconsideration.* Pennsylvania State UP, 1960.

Following the group presentations, I will lead a short class discussion on the NSLR. Our discussion will return to the four question clusters listed in the task itself (see Lesson 2: Group Task 1).

Through our discussion, we will come to realize that NSLRs can be prone to various logical fallacies and cognitive biases, primarily because the researcher does not have to document, or in any way rationalize, the research process. Some logical fallacies that can hinder NSLRs—and indeed hinder the exemplar literature review by Author X—include the Texas sharpshooter (Author X picks and chooses evidence to fit an argument), appeal to authority (Author X relies on the statues of experts to support an argument), and circular reasoning (Author X arrives at the endpoint of an argument, and that endpoint rests on the argument's premise). One cognitive bias that weakens the NSLR excerpt above is confirmation bias (Author X selects evidence that supports a premise and discards evidence that counters the premise).

Considering various shortcomings of the exemplar literature review excerpt, we will return to the convoluted nature of Margot's culpability in the shooting of her husband. While the author of the exemplar literature review asserts that Margot is guilty, appealing to authority along the way, Hemingway's text offers a scenario that is far less certain. Following this class discussion, we will move on to Group Task 2.

Lesson 2: Group Task 2

Earlier today, you worked in a group to examine and critique an excerpt of an NSLR on "Macomber." In carrying out that task, you identified a variety of drawbacks associated with the NSLR process (i.e., unclear research question, unclear research design, lack of transparency, issues of logical fallacies, cognitive biases, etc.). Working with the same group, you will now examine an excerpt of a rather different literature review, and again you will critique what you read.

Examine the demonstration literature review excerpt below. I have created it as a second exemplar for you to critique. Let's say it was written by Author Y. Carefully read the excerpt and, working with your group mates, answer three of the four question clusters below.

Subsequently, you will then share your findings with the class in a brief presentation that runs at approximately four to six minutes. Determine who will say what beforehand so that all group members know how they will contribute. I will circulate, monitor, and provide constructive feedback as you complete Group Task 2.

1. What is the research question (or set of questions) at the heart of Literature Review 2? What indicates this?

2. What are some key differences between Literature Review 2 and the one you previously examined? In other words, how does Author Y take a different approach than Author X? What would you say is striking about these differences?

3. How would you describe this literature review in terms of its logistics (i.e., gathering and selecting literature to be examined, use of search engines, etc.)?

4. If the previous literature review excerpt is an NSLR and this is one is an SLR, how would you differentiate between the two? What are some benefits and drawbacks associated with the SLR?

Literature Review 2 (Excerpt)

By Author Y

While much was written on "The Short Happy Life of Francis Macomber" between the 1950s and early 2000s, examining the current body of scholarship on the story has much to offer. It not only helps us to deepen our understanding of the narrative, but it also helps us to identify current trends and concerns in Hemingway and literary scholarship itself. As such, this systematic literature review (SLR) aims to address the following research questions: What does current scholarship say about Hemingway's 1936 story, "Macomber"? What are the patterns and possible gaps in this body of literature? What does this pool of research indicate about larger trends in the writing on Hemingway and literary scholarship itself?

It is important to begin with some definitions and parameters. For the purposes of this SLR, current scholarship is defined as peer-reviewed studies published over the last decade. Because books often go through a peer-review process—albeit not a blinded one—this SLR will include journal articles, book chapters, and books themselves. Also, because my aim is to focus on scholarship on "Macomber," I will exclude literary studies that mention the story in a cursory way. For a work of analysis to be included in this SLR, it needs to focus on the story at hand. Another aspect of the inclusion/exclusion criteria for this SLR relates to language. Only scholarship written in English is included in this SLR.

Two search engines were used for the initial searches, namely Google Scholar and ProQuest's MLA International Bibliography. In terms of keywords, the title of the story placed inside quotation marks was input into each search engine with the timeline set for 2008–2018. While the Google Scholar search yielded 493 results, the MLA International Bibliography search generated 19 results. Applying the inclusion/exclusion criteria to each list reduced the numbers to 16 and 8 respectively. Because 6 works appeared on both lists, I was left with a total of 18 articles, chapters, and books.

Drawing from critical theory, I examined each of the eighteen items with the following question in mind: What does current scholarship say about "Macomber" in relation to power systems and social conditions? Conducting a content analysis with this question in mind then led me to identify the following key themes: gender roles, racial identity, and consumerism/socioeconomic status. While eleven items explored the topic of gender roles (see Armengol-Carrera; Brandt and Renfroe; Fike; Godfrey; Hays; Khorsand and Ghasemi; Lamb; Mandel; Mohan; Monteiro; Wheeler), seven discussed racial identity (see Armengol-Carrera; duCille; Dudley; Kitunda; Larson; Mandel; Strong), and five considered the matter of consumerism/socioeconomic status (see Fike; Hays; Kitunda; Larson; Pingelton).

Surprisingly, very few scholars in this pool drew from an ecocritical perspective (see Godfrey; Harrington; McGill). Consequently, a discussion of each of the three major themes as well as the ecocriticism gap follows. We will not only consider what scholars say about the three core topics and gap, but we will also reflect on what these patterns mean.

REFERENCES—LITERATURE REVIEW 2 (EXCERPT)

Armengol-Carrera, Josep M. "Rac-ing Hemingway: Revisions of Masculinity and/as Whiteness in Ernest Hemingway's Green Hills of Africa and Under Kilimanjaro." *Hemingway Review,* vol. 31, no. 1, 2011, pp. 43–61.

Brandt, Kenneth K., and Alicia Mischa Renfroe. "Intent and Culpability: A Legal Review of the Shooting in 'The Short Happy Life of Francis Macomber.'" *Hemingway Review,* vol. 33, no. 2, 2014, pp. 8–29.

duCille, Ann. "The Short Happy Life of Black Feminist Theory." *differences,* vol. 21, no. 1, 2010, pp. 32–47.

Dudley, Marc K. *Hemingway, Race, and Art: Bloodlines and the Color Line.* Kent State UP, 2012.

Fike, Matthew A. "Hemingway's Francis Macomber in 'God's Country.'" *Journal of Jungian Scholarly Studies,* vol. 9, no. 5, 2014, 1–23.

Godfrey, Laura Gruber. "Text and Image: The Internet Generation Reads 'The Short Happy Life of Francis Macomber.'" *Hemingway Review,* vol. 32, no. 1, 2012, 39–56.

Hays, Peter L. *Fifty Years of Hemingway Criticism.* Scarecrow Press, 2014.

Harrington, Gary. "'Shootism' Versus 'Sport' in Hemingway's 'Macomber.'" *Teaching Hemingway and the Natural World,* edited by Kevin Maier, Kent State UP, 2017, pp. 137–48.

Kitunda, Jeremiah M. "'Love is a dunghill . . . And I'm the cock that gets on it to crow': Ernest Hemingway's Farcical Adoration of Africa." *Hemingway and Africa,* edited by Miriam B. Mandel, Camden House, 2011, pp. 122–50.

Khorsand, Golbarg, and Parvin Ghasemi. "Two Short Stories, Two Novels: An Examination of the Concept of Code Hero in Hemingway's Short and Long Fictions." *Analele Ştiinţifice ale Universităţii Ovidius din Constanţa. Seria Filologie,* vol. 24, no. 2, 2013, pp. 34–41.

Lamb, Robert Paul. *Art Matters: Hemingway, Craft, and the Creation of the Modern Short Story.* Louisiana State UP, 2010.

Larson, Kelli A. "On Safari with Hemingway: Tracking the Most Recent Scholarship." *Hemingway and Africa,* edited by Miriam B. Mandel, Camden House, 2011, pp. 323–81.

McGill, Christopher. "A Reading of Zoomoorphism in 'The Short Happy Life of Francis Macomber.'" *Explicator,* vol. 70, no. 1, 2012, pp. 57–60.

Mohan, B. "Hemingway's Female Characters—A Glance." *Asian Journal of Multidimensional Research,* vol. 2, no. 7, 2013, pp. 79–85.

Monteiro, George. *The Hemingway Short Story: A Critical Appreciation.* McFarland, 2017.

Pingelton, Timothy J. *Reading and Interpreting the Works of Ernest Hemingway.* Enslow, 2018.

Strong, Amy L. *Race and Identity in Hemingway's Fiction.* Palgrave MacMillan, 2008.

Unseth, Peter, and Georgi Kapchits. "Hemingway's Somali Proverb Confirmed. *ANQ: A Quarterly Journal of Short Articles, Notes and Reviews,* vol. 30, no. 4, 2017, pp. 253–54.

Wheeler, Belinda. "Redeeming Hemingway and His Women: Periodicals as Sites of Change in the Literature." *Teaching Hemingway and Gender,* edited by Verna Kale, Kent State UP, 2016, pp. 47–57.

Following presentations of Group Task 2, I will use the exemplar literature review by Author Y to lead a class discussion on the SLR. Through our discussion, we will note that conducting an SLR is a procedure of gathering a pool of research that is targeted to a certain research question (or set of questions). We will also note that once a suitable pool of research has been gathered, it is then necessary to examine, code, and analyze it. As our class discussion unfolds, it will be important to explore some (but not necessarily all) of the following questions:

- How can we form a suitable research question?
- What sorts of research questions would lead us to conduct an SLR?
- How can we set appropriate search parameters for an SLR (i.e., selecting search engines, journals, etc.)?
- How can we set suitable inclusion/exclusion criteria for an SLR?

Students will come to realize that while there is a procedure to conducting an SLR, the nuances of that procedure may differ from one SLR to another, depending on the core research questions at hand.

In closing this lesson, I will share some information about our five upcoming lessons. In the next lesson, we will delve into the practices of coding and analyzing a pool of research using such strategies as content analysis. The subsequent lesson will consider various types of SLRs (integrative and theoretical) as well as categories within SLRs (i.e., coverage, synthesis, methodology, significance, and rhetoric) (see Boote and Beile; Evans and Kowanko). The fifth, sixth, and seventh lessons of this sequence will involve a small project that will be completed both in and out of class. For this project, students will work in small groups to craft an SLR-oriented research question (or question set). They will then set parameters for their SLR (i.e., search and selection, coding and analysis) providing clear rationales along the way to support their research design. To supplement their research design, each group may draw from *Cooper's Taxonomy of Literature Reviews* to outline their purpose and process—attending to their literature review's focus, goal, perspective, coverage, organization, and audience (see Randolph). As a culminating project, groups will present their SLR parameters to the class and submit a written summary (1,500 to 2,000 words).

Conclusion

Teaching students how to conduct a rigorous literature review is both challenging and rewarding. Yet it is worth the effort. After all, there is much that the SLR offers budding scholars, as they navigate a vast, ever-expanding universe of literary scholarship. For students to develop and hone their skills in this area of scholarship they need to understand the nuances of forming a robust research question (or question set), and then mapping out a suitable research design, which includes setting search and selection criteria and planning steps for analyzing a body of scholarship. As previously mentioned, the SLR is particularly useful when using Hemingway in the classroom because so much has been written about his work. And "Macomber" is an exceptional candidate for introducing the SLR to students. As Larson recently noted, "The frequently anthologized 'The Short Happy Life of Francis Macomber' remains at the top of the critical stakes in the short story genre, resting comfortably in that position since the 1970s" (324).

In this chapter I have mapped out a way of introducing the SLR to a class, encouraging student voice and agency along the way. My approach has drawn from constructivism, student engagement, and critical pedagogy. Yet the strategies and timeline I have put forward are relevant for the *teaching-learning context* I described at the outset of this chapter. Of course, your own context will differ. As you reflect and plan for your own students, please feel free to tinker and adjust the learning activities I have put forward.

Works Cited

Boote, David N., and Penny Beile. "On the Centrality of the Dissertation of Literature Review in Research Preparation." *Educational Researcher,* vol. 34, no. 6, 2005, pp. 3–15.

Burbules, Nicholas C., and Rupert Berk. "Critical Thinking and Critical Pedagogy: Relations, Differences, and Limits." *Critical Theories in Education,* edited by Thomas S. Popkewitz and Lynn Fendler, Routledge, 1999, pp. 45–66.

Creswell, John W. *Qualitative Inquiry and Research Design: Choosing among Five Approaches.* Sage Publications, 2007.

Cruise, Adam. "The Effects of Trophy Hunting on Five of Africa's Iconic Wild Animal Populations in Six Countries: Analysis." Conservation Action Trust, Jan. 2016, https://conservationaction.co.za/resources/reports/effects-trophy-hunting-five-africas-iconic-wild-animal-populations-six-countries-analysis/.

Dewey, John. *Experience and Education.* Simon and Schuster, 1938.

"Elephant Hunting in Africa, 1930s." *YouTube,* uploaded by Huntley Films Archive, 23 Oct. 2017, https://www.youtube.com/watch?v=-4rYNWv8NUA.

Evans, David, and Inge Kowanko. "Literature Reviews: Evolution of a Research Methodology." *Australian Journal of Advanced Nursing,* vol. 18, no. 2, 2000, pp. 33–38.

Freire, Paulo. *Pedagogy of the Oppressed,* translated by M. B. Ramos, Continuum International, 2000.

Hmelo-Silver, Cindy E., et al. "Scaffolding and Achievement in Problem-Based and Inquiry Learning: A Response to Kirschner, Sweller, and Clark (2006)." *Educational Psychology,* vol. 42, no. 2, 2007, 99–107.

"Holiday Like Hemingway in Africa." Messy Nessy: Cabinet of Chic Curiosities, 2 Aug.
　　2017, http://www.messynessychic.com/2017/08/02/holiday-like-hemingway-in-africa/.
Lombard, Louisa. "Blame War, Not Safaris." *New York Times,* 29 June 2014, https://
　　www.nytimes.com/2014/06/30/opinion/blame-war-not-safaris.html.
Randolph, Justus J. "A Guide to Writing the Dissertation Literature Review." *Practical*
　　Assessment, Research and Evaluation, vol. 14, no. 13, 2009, 1–13.
Tyson, Lois. *Critical Theory Today: A User-Friendly Guide.* Routledge, 2015.

Reality TV in the Virtual Classroom

Teaching Hemingway's Canceled Episodes

("The Last Good Country")

Patrick Bonds

I include Hemingway's short stories in every online course I teach because reading Hemingway's shorter works requires critical reading practices that train students to become more active participants in their own life experiences. Ironically, my approach to such a towering task is to introduce (mostly) uninitiated Hemingway readers to the author's *unfinished* fiction—and I use reality television as a contextual aid. Reality TV, given its popularity with adolescents and older viewers alike, can serve as a basis for classroom discussion of the basic issues of reality and experience. Whereas students usually arrive equipped with an already keen visual literacy, reality TV provides an opportunity to analyze edited or shaped "reality" and its equivalent in quality fiction. The purpose and process of teaching Hemingway's work-in-progress novella "The Last Good Country" alongside the Discovery Channel's hit series *Deadliest Catch* in the literature survey course is the subject of this essay.

I am always encouraged by students' ability to "read" and analyze visual images, so I introduce general interpretive questions about setting, conflict, and theme by viewing and discussing the title sequence of *Deadliest Catch* (the video clips I refer to can be found on YouTube). The show, which depicts real-life events aboard Alaskan fishing vessels, features an opening montage of breathtaking views of a rugged coastline and the tempestuous waters of the Bering Sea. Scene after captivating scene rivets the viewers' attention on the dangerously cold waters into which crab men might be thrown at any moment as they slide across decks awash with half-ton steel crab pots. Clearly, the marketing strategy of the show is preoccupied with the "deadly" nature of the industry, illustrated in panoramic views of rollicking Bering Sea boats in treacherous weather conditions and intimate close-ups of bloody work injuries. Working in groups, the students look closely at still-frame images from the title sequence and discuss how each image evokes an emotional response. A sense of danger is present in each image, reminding viewers that the work these men perform—one of the most lucrative jobs in the world—is also one of the deadliest. After viewing the opening sequence together, I ask students to re-view individually the title sequence clip and at least one full-length episode, logging their emotional responses. The grinding, risky enterprise performed by real workers is, of course, part of the show's appeal, but on this point more sophisticated students will most likely announce that this "authenticity" is already undermined by the producers' insistence on the deadly aspects of the work, cashing in, so to speak, on danger and the possibility of injury or death. As with any reality show, of course, viewers witness only a stylized, edited version of the creators' and producers' "reality."

In the context of authenticity, I ask about the show's popularity, questioning whether the men on the crab vessels mirror many of the real-life struggles of the American working class and discussing how the show depicts everyday work alongside such themes as the importance of family, a strong work ethic, competition, and trying to make a living. Are all these values, I ask, inherent in the concept of the American Dream? If so, how can the show's narrative of hard work and American values be read as a reflection of an American cultural consciousness? Finally, I ask students to consider a remark made by Sig Hansen, one of the more prominent captains featured on the series, when asked to speculate about why the series is so popular: "*Catch*'s three million primarily male fans are drawn to the series much as they are to Westerns. We're the last of the cowboys," he says, "You get to do your own thing, make your own decisions, go where you want to go and do what you want to do" (Johnson). Before directing our attention to one of Hemingway's "unscripted" fictional texts— that is, incomplete, unpolished, and unpublished in his lifetime—we pause to consider Captain Hansen's statement, correlating the value of autonomy and its position in the process of American mythmaking.

From the Bering Sea, it is a short conceptual distance to Hemingway's northern Michigan as students quickly make a connection between the two frontier settings. We spend time discussing the landscape in "The Last Good Country" and compare how Hemingway's text and the *Deadliest Catch* series draw on a tradition of American Romanticism—an impulse to escape from the restraints and corruption of "civilization" to an unspoiled territory. We also contrast the emphasis on mortality (the Bering Sea boat crew, the armed wardens hunting Nick, and Nick's desire to kill the Evans boy) suggested by the constant undercurrent of danger. Somewhere along here I mention how these narratives suggest a kind of doomed utopia—hinted at explicitly in the playful Greek etymology of Hemingway's title "The Last Good Country": *ou-topos* ("no-place") and *eu-topos* ("good place"). The suggested tension between the real and the ideal provides a useful rubric: what does civilization do to wildness—and to autonomous life—in a world increasingly circumscribed by a rage for order and captivity?

Nick's sister, Littless, deserves special attention. Here we revisit the *Deadliest Catch* narrative and analyze the gendered role of the initiate, or "greenhorn," figure. In a traditional model, according to gender historian Michael Kimmel, the natural environment provides a male proving ground secured along the lines of three activities—not being characterized as feminine, seeking approval of other men, and banding together with other men. In this view, Littless's probing questions ("When is a man grown up?" [517]) and masculine "perfor-mance" (cutting her hair short "like a boy"; aping Nick's posture to "practic[e] being a boy" [531–33]) raises fascinating questions concerning gender identity and how selective symbols of masculinity are displayed and reproduced. I find that a rhetorical analysis approach to gender questions, using reality TV in all its complexity, is both engaging and instructive. Reality TV participants are very much aware of the fact that they are being filmed, which raises the basic question of whether participants are "playing to the camera"—behaving in a manner that they assume is consistent with the drama, roles, language, and norms of a television show, assumptions based on their knowledge of the medium. To what extent, I ask, can gender identity, like reality TV, be viewed as participants simply participating in a "fictional" drama based on predeter-mined scripts and roles?

I usually assign the deleted opening to "Indian Camp" (posthumously pub-lished as "Three Shots") as a companion study, comparing Littless and Nick as initiate figures in order to further develop the contrast between Nick's first failure of nerve in "Three Shots" and Littless's quest for maturity. How will Littless's wilderness education with Nick end? Because the text is unfinished, students feel less resistance supplying viable endings based on the setting, characters, and conflicts as they have come to understand them; in fact, the critical process of writing an end to the story based on the extant textual "evidence" is often cited in student discussions and evaluations as one of the most interesting and useful exercises in the course. I often cite the Nick Adams stories "Indian Camp" and "The Doctor and the Doctor's Wife" as examples of resonant but explicitly inconclusive endings. I find that the work we have done speculating about possible conclusions for "The Last Good Country" prepares students for the more challenging task of interpreting Hemingway's modernist endings that resist a sense of full closure or complete resolution.

Finally, we direct our attention full circle to issues of reality and experience and how "shaped" or "crafted" reality functions to intensify or interpret otherwise overlooked or misunderstood aspects of our own life experiences. Whether attending to questions of gender identity, the significance of work and family, or the timeless conflict of mortality, "unscripted" and "unedited" reality TV and its literary counterpart can provide a deadly combination for some killer classroom discussion.

Appendix: Handout on Character Archetypes

The character archetypes listed here are derived from Joseph Campbell's *The Hero with a Thousand Faces* and are deeply rooted in the myths and legends of many cultures.

Hero: The hero's journey during a story is a path from the ego, the self, to a new identity that has grown to include the experiences of the story. This path often consists of a separation from family or group to a new, unfamiliar, and challenging world (even one's own backyard), and finally a return to the ordinary, but now expanded, world. The hero must learn in order to grow. Often the heart of a story is not the obstacles he or she faces, but the new wisdom acquired from a mentor, a lover, or even from the villain. Heroes can be willing and adventurous or reluctant. They may be group and family oriented, or loners. They may change and grow themselves or act as catalysts for others to grow and act heroic. The hero can be an innocent, a wanderer, a martyr, a warrior, a vengeful destroyer, a ruler, or a fool. But the essence of the hero is the sacrifice he makes to achieve his goal.

Mentor: The mentor is a character who aids or trains the hero. The essence of the mentor is the wise old man or woman. The mentor represents the wiser and more godlike qualities within us. One major role of the mentor is to equip the hero by giving him gifts important to his quest. These gifts may be weapons, medicine or food, magic, or some important clue or piece of information. Frequently, the mentor requires the hero to have passed some sort of test before receiving the gift. The gift may be a seemingly insignificant object, the importance of which does not emerge until later.

Shadow: The shadow archetype is a negative figure, representing things we do not like and would like to eliminate. The shadow often takes the form of the antagonist in a story. But not all antagonists are villains; sometimes the antagonist is a good person whose goals conflict with the protagonist's. If the antagonist is a villain, though, he or she is a shadow. The shadow is the worthy opponent with whom the hero must struggle. In a conflict between hero and villain, the fight is to the end; one of them must be destroyed or rendered impotent. While the shadow is a negative force in the story, it is important to remember that no one is a villain in his or her own eyes. In fact, shadows frequently see themselves as heroes, and the story's hero as a villain.

Works Cited

Campbell, Joseph. *The Hero with a Thousand Faces.* Pantheon Books, 1949.

Hemingway, Ernest. "The Last Good Country." *The Complete Short Stories of Ernest Hemingway: The Finca Vigía Edition.* Scribner, 1991.

Johnson, Peter. "'Deadliest Catch' Survives High Seas, Lands Big Numbers." *USA Today,* 3 April 2007, p. 6D.

Kimmel, Michael. *Manhood in America: A Cultural History.* Free Press, 1997.

Contributors

John Beall is chair of the English Department at Collegiate School in New York City, where he has taught since 1989. His work has appeared in *MidAmerica*, the *Hemingway Review*, and the *James Joyce Quarterly*. In 2016 and 2017 he was awarded the Gwendolyn Brooks Poetry Prize by the Society for the Study of Midwestern Literature.

Patrick Bonds teaches at Troy University and has presented papers at the more recent international conferences of the Hemingway Society.

Janice F. Byrne, retired College of DuPage instructor and longtime teacher in Geneva, Illinois, specializes in the methodology for Ernest Hemingway's fiction. Her articles have appeared in a variety of journals and books, and her professional affiliations include the Hemingway Foundation and Society International, the Ernest Hemingway Foundation of Oak Park, and the Michigan Hemingway Society, where she sits on the board of directors.

Cam Cobb is associate professor in the Faculty of Education at the University of Windsor. He has been published in a variety of journals, including the *F. Scott Fitzgerald Review* and the *Hemingway Review,* and books, including *Per la Filosofia, Cinema: Philosophy and the Moving Image,* and *Hemingway and Italy: Twenty-First Century Perspectives.* With Marc Dudley, he is coeditor of the forthcoming *Hemingway and Film: Reflections on Teaching, Reading, and Understanding.*

Donald A. Daiker is professor emeritus of English at Miami University in Oxford, Ohio. He has joyfully taught classes on Hemingway in high schools, graduate seminars, corporate board rooms, and lifelong-learning programs. His two dozen Hemingway essays and reviews have appeared in the *Hemingway Review, Texas Studies in Literature and Language, North Dakota Quarterly,*

McNeese Review, Studies in Short Fiction, MidAmerica, Twentieth-Century Literature, South Atlantic Review, Middle West Review, and *Resources for American Literary Study.* He is a member of the editorial board of the *Hemingway Review.*

Marc Dudley is associate professor of English at North Carolina State University. He specializes in twentieth-century American literature, with particular emphasis on modern fiction and American culture. His primary scholarly concerns are issues of race and identity as they relate to notions of Americana. In *Hemingway, Race, and Art: Bloodlines and the Color Line,* he investigated Ernest Hemingway's rarely recognized lifelong interest in race. He is also the author of *Understanding James Baldwin.*

Peter L. Hays is professor emeritus at the University of California, Davis. His most recent book is *Reading Hemingway's* The Old Man and the Sea, cowritten with Bickford Sylvester and Larry Grimes.

Judy Siegel Henn recently retired after forty-seven years as an educator in English and in Hebrew, teaching every level from nursery school to PhD candidates. She received thirteen awards as Outstanding Lecturer from the Technion Student Association in Israel. She ended her teaching career by lecturing at the Chinese Technion–Guangdong Technion-Israel Institute of Technology.

Hilary Kovar Justice joined the John F. Kennedy Library Foundation in 2016 as Hemingway Program Specialist. Prior to joining the foundation, she was associate professor of English and director of undergraduate studies at Illinois State University. An award-winning scholar and educator, she has published extensively on Ernest Hemingway, including her 2006 book, *The Bones of the Others: The Hemingway Text from the Lost Manuscripts to the Posthumous Novels.* She has served on the boards of the Hemingway Society and the Ernest Hemingway Foundation of Oak Park and on the editorial board of the *Hemingway Review.*

Verna Kale is assistant research professor in English at Pennsylvania State University and associate editor of the Cambridge edition of *The Letters of Ernest Hemingway.* She has published a critical biography, *Ernest Hemingway,* and is editor of *Teaching Hemingway and Gender,* part of the Teaching Hemingway series (Kent State University Press, 2016). She has contributed to the *Hemingway Review,* the *Journal of Popular Culture,* the *Conversation, Ernest Hemingway in Context,* and *Hemingway and the Geography of Memory.*

Debra A. Moddelmog is a scholar and teacher of twentieth-century American literature, modernism, and sexuality studies. She is author of *Reading Desire: In Pursuit of Ernest Hemingway* and coeditor of *Ernest Hemingway in Context*. She is a member of the editorial board of the *Hemingway Review* and of the advisory board for the Hemingway Letters Project. She currently serves as dean of liberal arts at the University of Nevada, Reno.

Marc Seals is professor of English at the University of Wisconsin-Platteville Baraboo Sauk County, where he teaches courses in American literature, composition, and film. His scholarship has appeared in the *Hemingway Review, MidAmerica, Eureka Studies in Teaching Short Fiction, Miswestern Miscellany,* and *Twentieth-Century Literary Criticism.*

Frederic J. Svoboda has taught at the Flint campus of the University of Michigan since 1980, focusing on American literature and culture, and has served as both chair of English and director of the graduate program in American culture. He served as senior faculty advisor to UM–Flint's chancellor and as chair of Faculty Council, and he was elected to two terms as a board member and treasurer of the Ernest Hemingway Foundation. He also is a past president and current vice president of the Michigan Hemingway Society. A recent book, coedited with Suzanne del Gizzo, collected criticism of Hemingway's posthumously published novel *The Garden of Eden.*

Index